THE *ideals* AMERICAN COOKBOOK

The fragrance and the flavor lingers for a lifetime once you've tasted hush puppies of the South . . . stuffed lobsters of New England . . . persimmon pudding of the Middle West . . . salmon of the West . . . fruits from Hawaii and venison from Alaska.

. . . apple pie and baked beans, hot dogs and potato salad . . . and, recipes for all of these and more, are blended into our newest cookbook, the IDEALS AMERICAN COOKBOOK!

Some of these recipes were brought to our new country by our pioneer ancestors; some are specialties of a particular area of our great country; but all are alive with tradition . . . all delicious, different, but containing ingredients that are very familiar to us all.

And sprinkled here and there with a touch of poetry and a dash of beautiful photography and artwork, this is a book we are sure you will love to have in your cookbook library for your own constant use, and to give to many of your friends as gifts.

. . . for when we share of ourselves, and our cooking, we are truly giving of ourselves in the best of American traditions!

managing editor
Ralph Luedtke

contributing editor
Lorraine Obst

ISBN 0-89542-634-X 250
IDEALS PUBLISHING CORP., MILWAUKEE, WIS. 53201
© COPYRIGHT MCMLXXVI, PRINTED AND BOUND IN U.S.A.

Fourth Printing

CONTENTS

NORTHEAST 3

SOUTHEAST 14

NORTH CENTRAL .26

SOUTH CENTRAL .37

WEST 48

HAWAII 59

ALASKA 61

VOICE OF AMERICA

I am the cornfields of the Middle West,
Rustling and whispering in the prairie
    breeze;
The snowcapped Rockies pointing to the sky.
I am youth's ambitions: symbols of these . . .

The cottonfields and bluegrass of the South
That stand for gracious hospitality;
The spirit of undefeated statehood
And antebellum aristocracy.

I am the rolling voice of crested waves
Inviting all within my golden gate;
The vast Pacific of the vibrant West,
With shore and climate sure to captivate.

I am America! Its eastern towns,
Its rocky hillsides and its winding streams,
With torch to light the pathway to their
    dreams!

Stella Craft Tremble

ABBREVIATIONS

t. — teaspoon
T — tablespoon
c. — cup
pkg. — package
pt. — pint
qt. — quart
oz. — ounce
lb. — pound

MAINE

VERMONT

NEW HAMPSHIRE

MASSACHUSETTS

CONNECTICUT

RHODE ISLAND

NEW YORK

NEW JERSEY

PENNSYLVANIA

Pennsylvania Dutch Chowder
Cranberry Pie

PENNSYLVANIA DUTCH CHOWDER

½ c. sliced celery
½ c. chopped onion
2 T. butter or margarine
2 10½-oz. cans condensed
   chicken 'n dumplings soup
1½ soup cans water
1 8-oz. can whole kernel corn
   Pepper to taste

Cook celery and onion in butter until tender. Add the remaining ingredients. Heat, stirring the chowder now and then. Makes 4 to 6 servings.

POTATO SOUP

2 c. potatoes, sliced
¼ c. chopped onion
1¼ c. boiling water
1½ c. milk
1 T. margarine
1 t. salt
   Pepper

Cook potatoes and onion in water until tender. Mash potatoes slightly. Add milk, fat, and seasonings. Heat and serve. Garnish with chopped parsley.

NEW ENGLAND BAKED BEANS

2 lbs. beans (yellow eye, red kidney,
   or small pea beans)
1 t. baking soda
1½ c. maple syrup or 12 T. brown sugar
1 onion, chopped
2 t. salt
½ lb. lean salt pork cut into 1-inch pieces
½ t. dry mustard
3 T. molasses
¼ t. ginger
1 small pinch of ground cloves

Place beans in large cooking pot and cover them with water—let soak overnight. In the morning, in same pot simmer for 5 to 10 minutes. Add 1 t. baking soda. Water will foam and turn yellow. Rinse beans thoroughly and put into large bean pot. Add remaining ingredients and cover with water. Bake at 300° for 6 hours. Check beans every hour and add more water when needed.

Ginger Williams

BROWN BREAD

⅔ c. molasses
1 c. rye or graham flour
1 c. cornmeal
1 c. white flour
1 t. salt
1 t. baking soda
½ c. raisins
½ c. buttermilk (if necessary,
   add a little more to mix well)

Put in covered dish and steam for 3 hours.

Avis A. Croteau

4

DEVILED CRAB

3 c. crabmeat, fresh or canned
2 eggs
½ c. milk
1 T. Worcestershire sauce
1 small onion, grated
1 green pepper, finely chopped
½ c. butter
2 c. crumbs or saltines
½ t. salt
1 t. chopped green pepper

Preheat oven to 325°. Mix crabmeat with other ingredients. Pack mixture into buttered ramekins or crab shells. Sprinkle with butter and cracker crumbs. Bake until brown, about 15 to 20 minutes.

Mildred King

ESCALLOPED OYSTERS

1 pt. fresh oysters
¼ lb. butter or margarine, melted
2 c. crushed soda crackers
Salt and pepper to taste
½ c. milk

Mix butter and cracker crumbs, salt and pepper.

Arrange a layer of cracker mixture in casserole, then a layer of oysters, and alternate, ending with crumb mixture. Add milk. Bake at 350° for about 45 minutes.

Mrs. William Woods

I love the old white farmhouses nestled
  in New England valleys,
Ample and long and low, with elm trees
  bending above them . . .
Borders of box in the yard, and lilacs
  and old-fashioned flowers,
A fanlight over the door and little
  square panes in the windows,
The woodshed piled with maple and
  birch and hickory ready for winter,
The gambrel roof with its garret crowded
  with household relics—
All the tokens of prudent thrift and the
  spirit of self-reliance . . .

Author Unknown

NEW ENGLAND FISH CHOWDER

1 lb. fish fillets, fresh or frozen
2 T. chopped bacon or salt pork
½ c. chopped onion
2½ c. diced raw potatoes
1½ c. boiling water
1 t. salt
Pepper to taste
2 c. milk
1 T. butter
Chopped parsley

Thaw frozen fish and remove the skin and bones. Cut fish into 1-inch pieces.

Fry bacon or salt pork in a large saucepan until crisp. Add onion and cook until tender. Add potatoes, water, salt, pepper and fish. Cover. Simmer until potatoes are tender.

Add milk and butter. Heat. Garnish with parsley.

SCALLOP CASSEROLE

1 lb. fresh or frozen scallops
2 T. butter
2 T. flour
2 c. milk
½ c. sliced celery
¼ c. diced pimiento
¼ t. salt
Dash pepper
½ c. fine bread crumbs
2 T. melted butter

Wash fresh scallops (or defrost frozen scallops). Melt 2 T. butter, blend in flour and cook until smooth, then gradually add the milk. Simmer until mixture thickens.

Mix scallops, celery, pimiento, salt and pepper. Place in casserole, pour in the white sauce. Mix the bread crumbs and melted butter, and spoon around the edge of casserole. Bake in a 350° oven about 30 minutes. Garnish with lemon.

HALIBUT AMANDINE

5 halibut steaks	½ c. milk
3 T. butter	2 T. lemon juice
2 T. flour	2 beaten egg yolks
½ t. salt	2 T. sliced almonds
Dash pepper	

Cover steaks in water in a heavy cast iron type frying pan. Simmer about 5 to 10 minutes or until fish flakes easily. Drain the fish, reserving 1 cup of the liquid. Keep steaks warm.

Melt butter in pan; stir in flour, salt and pepper. Add reserved liquid, cooking until bubbly. Stir in lemon juice.

Stir small amount of hot mixture into eggs and milk, then return to hot mixture in pan. Cook just a bit longer until completely warmed.

Pour over steaks. Sprinkle with almonds.

Patricia Dodson

CORN OYSTERS

Corn oysters are an old-time dish
We shouldn't let pass by,
So try this simple recipe
And you will find out why:

Mix one cup corn...whole kernel style,
With one-fourth cup of flour
And add an egg that's beaten up
And stir together well.

Then salt and pepper it to taste
And shape in oyster size,
And when you've fried them in hot fat,
You'll really have a prize.

Make sure your fat is good and hot
Before you start to fry.
I'll bet you'll make them oftentimes
As in the days gone by.

Craig E. Sathoff

STUFFED BAKED LOBSTER

Allow one small lobster per person.

Boil lobster, drain, and plunge into cold water. Split and clean it. (Directions for boiling lobster may be found below.)

STUFFING

2 c. finely crushed crackers	
½ c. melted butter	
Pepper	
2½ T. Worcestershire sauce	
Melted butter	

Toss together the cracker crumbs, ½ c. melted butter, pepper and Worcestershire sauce. Spoon stuffing lightly into lobster shell.

Heat oven to 375° and bake for 35 minutes.

Serve with melted butter.

★ ★ ★

To boil a lobster—have a large kettle of briskly boiling water. Add 1 tablespoon salt to 1 quart of water. Pick up live lobster behind its head, or use tongs, if desired. Let water return to boiling after the addition of each lobster—then cover the kettle and boil for about 10 minutes for a small lobster. The shell will be bright red. Do not overcook or the flesh will be tough.

Let cool and proceed as above for stuffed lobster.

BAKED CORN

3 eggs, separated	
½ c. evaporated milk, undiluted	
1 t. salt	
3 T. sugar	
1½ T. flour	
2 c. cooked or canned corn	
2 T. melted butter	

Beat egg yolks; add milk, salt, sugar, flour, corn and melted butter. Fold in stiffly beaten egg whites and pour into greased casserole. Bake in a 300° oven for 40 to 45 minutes.

This is very delicious. Can be made ahead and put in oven just before dinner.

Ruth Sprenkle

Baked corn
Stuffed Baked Lobster

CHICKEN PAPRIKA WITH SPAETZLES

¼ c. margarine
1 medium onion, chopped
3 c. water
2 chicken bouillon cubes
   Salt and pepper to taste
2 T. paprika
1 frying chicken, cut up

Put margarine in a large kettle. Sauté onion. Add remaining ingredients. Simmer until chicken is tender but still on bones. Remove chicken from broth. Thicken broth with a flour and water mixture. Place 1 pint of sour cream into a bowl, then add several spoonfuls of hot broth and stir. Add entire mixture to hot broth. Add chicken and keep warm until ready to serve. Add 1 clove mashed garlic for more flavor if desired.

SPAETZLES

6 eggs
1 t. salt
2½ c. flour

Mix above ingredients together to form a very soft dough. Place part of the dough onto a saucer. With a moistened spoon cut off small part of dough and drop into a kettle of unsalted boiling water. Continue until all dough is used from saucer. When the spaetzles float, cook several more minutes. Continue this process until all dough is used. Keep hot over boiling water.

Linda S. Derrick

NEW ENGLAND CARROT STEAMED PUDDING

1 c. ground raw carrot
1 c. ground raw potato
1 t. baking soda
1 c. sugar
2 T. shortening
1 egg
1 c. flour
1 t. salt
½ t. cinnamon
½ t. nutmeg
1 c. raisins
2 small cans candied fruit

Mix all together and steam in double boiler pan for 3 hours or cook 40 minutes in pressure cooker in coffee can if desired.

May be stored or frozen in foil and reheated in it.

Mrs. Kermit Stevens

NEW ENGLAND PLUM PUDDING

Soak 1 pound package soda crackers in water, then squeeze dry. Add:

1 c. milk	½ c. raisins
1 c. molasses	Salt
3 T. melted butter	2 beaten eggs
½ t. cinnamon	½ c. sugar
¼ t. nutmeg	

If desired, dates may be added. Bake in 350° oven until firm. Slice and serve with hard sauce or whipped cream. Also delicious served cold.

Mrs. Julius Abegg

NEW ENGLAND MOLASSES CAKE

½ c. shortening
½ c. sugar
1 egg
2½ c. flour
1 t. cinnamon
1 t. cloves
½ t. salt
1 t. baking soda dissolved
   in 1 c. buttermilk
1 c. molasses

Cream shortening and sugar, add egg. Alternately add the flour, sifted with salt and spices, the buttermilk, soda and molasses.

Bake in greased pan at 350° until done.

Mrs. Bryan McCallum

LEMON BREAD PUDDING

3 slices dry bread, cubed
3¼ c. sugar (Reserve ¼ c. to be used later)
3 c. milk
  Grated rind of one lemon
⅛ t. salt
3 egg yolks (Reserve whites)
1 t. lemon extract

Combine all ingredients and set baking dish in pan of water in a 375° oven.

Stir gently from outside to center once after it begins to cook. When slightly cooked or thickened (which takes at least 30 minutes), pour over it the 3 beaten egg whites to which has been added the juice of 1 lemon and the ¼ cup sugar. If the lemon is not very juicy, use more. Return to oven and when it coats a knife, it is done.

Orange can be used in place of lemon, or they can be mixed. 6 to 8 servings.

Evelyn Fletcher

MAPLE PUDDING

¾ c. maple syrup
3 slices bread. Remove crusts
1 T. softened butter or margarine
½ c. seedless raisins
½ t. grated lemon rind
2 c. milk
2 eggs
  Pinch of salt
⅛ t. vanilla

Pour the maple syrup into top of a double boiler. Spread bread with the softened butter, cut in cubes and add to the maple syrup. Place raisins and lemon rind over top. Beat together the eggs, milk, salt and vanilla and pour over bread mixture. Do not stir. Set over gently boiling water, cover and cook 1 hour. The sauce that forms under the custardy pudding should be spooned over each serving. Serve warm. Serves 6.

MAMA'S MOLASSES CAKES

1 c. butter or margarine
1 c. sugar
1 egg
1 c. molasses
4¾ c. flour (sifted)
3 t. baking soda
½ t. salt
1 t. instant coffee powder
  (Mama used strong coffee)
¾ t. ginger
1½ t. cinnamon
¾ c. boiling water

Cream butter or margarine until light. Add sugar and beat until fluffy. Beat in egg and mix thoroughly. Blend in molasses. Add coffee powder to boiling water. Sift dry ingredients together and add to creamed mixture alternately with coffee. Mix until well blended.

Drop by heaping teaspoonfuls 2 inches apart on greased cookie sheet. Bake at 375° for 12 to 15 minutes. Cool on racks. Makes 5 dozen.

Mrs. J. Raynor Powell

APPLE CHIP CAKE

1⅓ c. salad oil
2 c. sugar
2 eggs
3 c. apples peeled and cut in chunks
1 c. chopped nuts
½ t. salt
1 t. baking soda
1 t. cinnamon
1 t. vanilla
3 c. sifted flour

Blend the salad oil, sugar and eggs. Add the remaining ingredients in the order given. Batter will be stiff.

Spoon into oblong pan or 2 9-inch cake pans. Do not grease pans. Bake at 350° for 1 hour.

Louise Hanicker

NUT COOKIES

1 lb. black walnut meats
4 egg whites
2 c. granulated sugar
2 T. flour (heaping)

Beat egg whites until very stiff. Then, very gradually add sugar, then flour. Fold in nuts.

Grease cookie sheets with butter. With two spoons, make small kisses. Bake at 350° for 12 minutes. Let cool in pans before removing.

Mrs. William N. Robey

9

APPLE COBBLER

⅔ c. sugar
3 T. quick-cooking tapioca
⅛ t. salt
1½ c. water
5 c. tart, pared apple slices
⅓ c. milk
1 c. biscuit mix
2 T. butter or margarine, melted
¼ c. sugar
1 t. cinnamon

Mix sugar, tapioca, salt and water in a large saucepan. Let stand while preparing apple slices. Then bring tapioca mixture to a full boil, stirring to prevent sticking. Add apples. Cover and boil gently until apples are tender, 10 to 15 minutes. Stir occasionally to prevent sticking. Pour tapioca and apples into a 9-inch square pan.

Stir milk into biscuit mix. Roll dough to 6 x 10-inch rectangle. Spread dough with the 2 T. butter and sprinkle with sugar and cinnamon. Roll as for a jelly roll, starting from short side. Cut dough into 12 slices ½-inch thick. Arrange on apple-tapioca mixture. Bake at 425° about 20 minutes or until biscuits are browned. Serve with cream or hot sauce.

Pauline Carter

NEVER-FAIL NUTBREAD

2 c. flour
¼ t. salt
2 t. baking powder
1 egg
1 c. sugar
1 c. milk
1 c. nuts, chopped, but not too fine

Sift flour, salt and baking powder. Beat egg and sugar together until creamy. Add dry ingredients alternately with milk. Add nuts. Pour batter into a loaf pan and bake at 300° for 50 minutes.

This nut bread becomes something extra special when served with a spread made by softening a 3-ounce package of cream cheese with juice from maraschino cherries and adding diced pieces of the cherries. Use only enough juice to make a good spreading consistency. For a Christmas treat make two batches of cheese spread, using red cherries in one batch and green cherries in the other.

Martha Cramer

MOLASSES PUMPKIN BREAD

⅓ c. shortening
1 c. sugar
2 eggs
½ c. light or dark molasses
1 c. mashed pumpkin
2 c. flour
¼ t. baking powder
1 t. baking soda
½ t. salt
2 t. pumpkin spice
1 c. coarsely chopped walnuts

Cream shortening; stir in sugar and eggs. Stir in molasses and pumpkin. Stir in the remaining ingredients and beat well. Bake in greased loaf pan for 1 hour or more at 350°. Turn out and cool on rack. Slice thinly, spread with butter or whipped cream cheese.

Mrs. Henry Jeppesen

FASTNACHTS
(Raised Doughnuts)

1 c. mashed potatoes
1¼ c. sugar
1 yeast cake (or 2 env. powdered yeast) soaked in lukewarm potato water

Set the above at 5:00 p.m. Then, about 10:30 p.m. add:

1 c. margarine
2 eggs, beaten
1¼ c. sugar
4 c. cold water
1 T. salt

In the morning add flour as for bread. When dough doesn't stick to hands there is enough flour. Knead. Place dough in bowl and let rise. Roll and cut out. Let rise again before frying in deep fat or oil.

Ruth Krug Dolbey

POPOVERS

3 eggs
1 c. milk
2 T. melted butter
1 c. flour
½ t. salt

Grease muffin tins and place them in an oven that is preheating at 450°.

Beat eggs well. Add milk and butter. Mix flour and salt; add to liquid mixture. Beat until smooth.

Fill hot muffin tins half full of batter. Bake at 450° for 15 minutes; reduce heat to 375° and bake 10 minutes longer. Do not open oven door during baking.

Immediately after baking, insert a paring knife through the top of each popover to allow steam to escape.

NEW ENGLAND PANCAKES

PANCAKES

2 c. pancake mix   1 egg
2 c. milk   2 T. melted butter

FILLING AND TOPPING

Melted butter
Shaved maple sugar
Whipped cream

Add milk, egg and butter to pancake mix, stirring lightly. A somewhat lumpy batter makes light, fluffy pancakes. For each pancake, pour ¼ cup batter onto a hot, lightly buttered griddle. Bake to a golden brown, turning only once. Stack 3 pancakes, placing melted butter and shaved maple sugar (or brown sugar) between each. Top with whipped cream and sprinkle with brown sugar. Makes 14 to 16 pancakes.

11

MAINE PUMPKIN PIE

Pastry for 1-crust pie

Filling:

1½ c. cooked pumpkin	½ t. salt
1½ c. milk	¾ t. cinnamon
2 eggs, beaten	¼ t. ginger
1 T. molasses	¼ t. cloves
¾ c. brown sugar	¼ t. nutmeg

Mix together all ingredients and place in an unbaked pie crust. Bake at 450° for 10 minutes, then reduce heat to 350° and bake 25 minutes or until a knife inserted in pie comes out clean.

Inez G. Files

SOUR CREAM PIE

1 c. sour cream	⅛ t. cloves
½ c. seeded raisins, chopped fine	1 c. sugar
¼ t. cinnamon	3 eggs, separated

To 3 egg yolks and white of 1 egg add sugar, spices, sour cream and raisins. Bake in an unbaked pie shell in a 350° oven until custard is set and almost done. Beat the 2 egg whites and 2 tablespoons of sugar until stiff. Then spread on top of pie and put back in oven to brown.

Miriam Staiger

MONTGOMERY PIE

Pastry for two 8-inch pies

Step 1:

1 lemon—juice and grated rind
1 egg, lightly beaten
1 c. sugar
1 c. water
½ c. molasses

Mix molasses, water with lemon. Add the egg and sugar. Pour into pie shells.

Step 2:

2 c. milk
2½ c. flour
2 t. baking powder

Mix thoroughly.

Spoon this mixture over first part of this recipe which is in the pie shells. Do not stir. Bake 30 minutes in 375° oven.

Mary A. Miller

PENNSYLVANIA DUTCH SHOO FLY PIE

CRUMB MIXTURE

½ c. butter
1½ c. flour
1 c. light brown sugar

Mix above together with hands.

LIQUID MIXTURE

1 c. molasses
1 egg, beaten
¾ c. boiling water
¾ t. baking soda

1 unbaked pie shell

Mix liquid mixture together. Pour into unbaked pie shell. Sprinkle crumb mixture on top of liquid mixture. Bake at 400° for 15 minutes. Reduce heat to 350°. Bake approximately 30 minutes more, or until mixture is set.

Mrs. Paul E. King

CRANBERRY PIE

Pictured on page 3

1 9-inch unbaked pie shell
2 c. cranberries
1 c. sugar
½ c. water
1 T. cornstarch
1 T. butter

Wash and pick over the cranberries. Cook the sugar and water 2 minutes, add the cranberries and cook for 5 minutes. Mix the cornstarch and the softened butter and add enough of the hot cranberry liquid to make a smooth paste. Stir this mixture into the simmering cranberries. Cook 3 minutes, stirring constantly. Pour the cranberry mixture into the pie shell. Cross with lattice top. Bake 10 to 15 minutes in a preheated oven at 450°. Reduce the heat to 350° and bake 25 to 30 minutes longer.

Apple Butter Pie   *Maple Syrup Pie*

MAPLE SYRUP PIE

1 baked pie shell

1 c. maple syrup	**1 t. butter**
1 c. hot water	**2 T. cornstarch**
2 eggs, separated	**⅛ t. salt**

Combine 1 cup syrup, hot water and butter. Bring to a full boil. Mix cornstarch, salt and enough cold water to make a thin paste. Add egg yolks to paste and beat well. Add hot syrup mixture gradually and return to heat. Cook until thickened, stirring constantly. Cool slightly. Pour into baked pie shell. Beat egg whites until stiff, slowly adding a tablespoon of syrup. Pile on pie and brown until golden in hot oven. Add chopped nuts if desired.

Ruth B. Field

APPLE BUTTER PIE

¾ c. apple butter	**1 T. flour, heaping**
1 egg	**2 c. milk**
½ c. sugar	**1 t. cinnamon**

Beat egg well. Add sugar and stir well. Add flour, apple butter, milk and cinnamon. Pour into pie shell. Bake like custard pie at 350° for about 1 hour.

Mrs. Jay W. Ziegler

SOUTHEAST

TENNESSEE

KENTUCKY

ALABAMA

DELAWARE   GEORGIA

MARYLAND   FLORIDA

WEST VIRGINIA   NORTH CAROLINA

VIRGINIA   SOUTH CAROLINA

QUICK PRALINE ROLLS

1 packet yeast softened in ¼ c. warm
  water

Sift into large mixing bowl:

2¼ c. flour
2 T. sugar
2 t. baking powder
½ t. salt

Cut in ⅓ c. butter or margarine until particles
are fine. Stir in ⅓ c. scalded milk cooled to
lukewarm. Add one unbeaten egg and the
softened yeast. Beat well. Toss on well-
floured surface and roll out to a 15 x 10-inch
rectangle.

FILLING

Cream ⅓ c. butter or margarine with ¾ c.
firmly packed brown sugar until fluffy.
Spread ½ of this sugar mixture over dough.
Sprinkle with ½ c. pecans, chopped. Roll up,
starting with 15-inch side, sealing the edge.
Cut into one-inch slices and place on greased
cookie sheet. Flatten with palm of hand,
spread with the remaining sugar mixture.
Sprinkle with more chopped pecans. Cover
and let rise in warm place about 45 minutes or
until light. Bake at 425° for 10 to 12 minutes.
May be frosted with a glaze while warm.
Makes about 2 dozen rolls.

Carol Lou Shanklin

SEAFOOD NEWBURG

4 T. butter
½ c. flour
6 c. milk
1½ t. salt
½ t. paprika
4 egg yolks
4 c. canned or cooked seafood
  (shrimp, lobster, crabmeat or tuna,
  cut in pieces)
2 T. sherry, optional

Melt butter in saucepan; blend in flour. Add
milk and cook, stirring constantly, until mixture thickens and comes to a boil. Add salt
and paprika. Quickly stir a small amount of
the hot mixture into slightly beaten egg yolks;
return to remaining sauce and cook 3 minutes
longer. Remove from heat; stir in seafood and
sherry. Heat to serving temperature. Serve
on toast.

DEVILED CRAB

1½ c. milk
1½ c. soft bread crumbs
2 c. flaked cooked crabmeat or
  2 7-oz. cans
5 hard-cooked eggs, sliced

Pick over crabmeat and discard any bits of
shell or cartilage. Stir crabmeat and hard-
cooked eggs into combined milk and bread
crumbs.

Blend in:

1½ t. salt
⅓ t. dry mustard
⅛ t. cayenne pepper
½ c. melted butter

Pour into buttered baking dish, sprinkle with
crumbs. Bake in a 400° oven for 15 minutes.
Serve hot. Makes 6 servings.

Ruth Sprenkle

IMPERIAL CRAB

1 lb. crabmeat
⅓ green pepper, chopped
1 small pimiento, chopped
1 egg
⅓ c. mayonnaise
¼ t. pepper
½ t. salt
1 t. dry mustard

Pick over crabmeat. Gently combine all ingredients and place in shells. Bake at 350° for
15 minutes. Serves 6.

Eleanor Brandt

BACKYARD CLAMBAKE

12 steamer clams
 1 1-lb. lobster
 ½ small broiler-fryer
 1 ear of corn
 1 potato, cut lengthwise in eighths

 1 small onion, quartered
 Salt and pepper
 Melted butter
 1 yard square cheesecloth
 Seaweed, if available

Scrub clams. Rinse and split lobster. Remove sharp bones from chicken. Shuck corn. Tear off large squares of heavy-duty foil and cover each with a cheesecloth square. If you have seaweed, put a handful on the cheesecloth; top with chicken, then lobster and clams. Tuck in corn, onion and potato wherever there is room. Salt and pepper to taste. If you haven't used seaweed, add 4 tablespoons water to each package. Tie cheesecloth up over the food, then close foil into airtight package. Place packages on grill over medium hot coals and cook 45 minutes to 1 hour. Open a package after 35 minutes to test chicken for doneness; if not tender, reclose and continue cooking. Melt butter and pour into individual dishes for each person.

CHARLESTON OKRA SOUP

1 large beef soupbone
2 medium onions, chopped
3 lbs. fresh okra, chopped fine
  Salt, pepper and bay leaf
3 qts. water
1 piece breakfast bacon
8 large fresh tomatoes,
  or 2 #2½ cans tomatoes

Wash meat and cook in water for 2 hours. Add okra, bacon, peeled tomatoes, onions, bay leaf and salt and pepper to taste. Let cook another 2 hours. Add more water if needed. Remove bay leaf.

Charlene Myers

ROOT BEER BREAD

2 pkgs. dry yeast	⅓ c. sugar
½ c. warm water	1 T. salt
1 t. sugar	¼ c. molasses
1 qt. root beer	2 c. rye flour
2 T. shortening	12 c. white flour

Dissolve yeast in warm water. Add 1 t. sugar and let stand a few minutes. Heat root beer slightly, add shortening and stir until melted. Add sugar, salt, molasses and yeast mixture. Then add rye flour, white flour until all flour is mixed in. Knead lightly, but do not over-knead. Let rise 2 hours, then punch down. Let rise again, about 1 hour. Divide dough into 4 parts and place in buttered pans. Let rise 45 minutes. Bake at 350° for 45 minutes.

James Lesniak

OVERNIGHT CASSEROLE

2 c. macaroni (uncooked)
¼ lb. shredded cheese
¼ lb. ground ham
2 cans cream of mushroom soup
4 eggs, hard-cooked and diced
1 onion, minced

Combine above ingredients. Let stand overnight. Bake in a 350° oven 1 hour.

Margaret Weiss

CHICKEN PIE

Clean and cut chicken. Boil until tender. Salt chicken while cooking to suit your own taste. When cooked, cool and take meat from bones and cut in small cubes. Use your favorite rich pie crust or pastry without baking powder. Roll one crust for the bottom and one for the top.

FILLING

1½ to 2 c. of diced chicken according to the size of your pan
  2 T. flour
    Black pepper lightly sprinkled on top
  1 to 1½ c. chicken broth

Place in unbaked pie shell. Cover with pastry top. Dampen the edge so top crust will adhere to bottom crust. Flute edges. Cut a cross in top of the pastry to permit steam to escape. Bake at 350° for 30 minutes or until pie has boiled up and the crust is brown. One chicken will make one pie.

Anne Krites

BAKED CHICKEN MARYLAND

2 2½-lb. frying chickens
1 c. flour
1 t. salt
½ t. pepper
1 egg
2 T. water
1½ c. coarse bread crumbs
⅓ c. butter or margarine
1 t. lemon juice
2 T. water

Butter a large casserole.

Cut chickens in pieces for serving, wash and dry.

Mix the flour, salt and pepper, and roll the chicken in it. Then dip each piece of chicken in the egg, beaten slightly, with the water, and roll each in the crumbs. Place in casserole.

Bake, uncovered, about 45 minutes or until tender, basting occasionally with the combined butter or margarine, lemon juice and water.

Remove to a hot serving dish. Serve with cream gravy.

BRUNSWICK STEW

1 medium onion, chopped
1 T. fat or oil
2 c. cooked or canned tomatoes
2 c. cooked or canned lima beans
2 c. cooked or canned corn
2 c. cut-up canned chicken or turkey
Salt and pepper

Cook onion in fat or oil in a large pan until tender. Drain vegetables. Add water to vegetable liquid to make 2 cups; add to onion. Add rest of ingredients. Heat just to boiling and serve.

EQUIVALENT MEASURES

3 teaspoons	equals 1 tablespoon
4 tablespoons	equals ¼ cup
16 tablespoons	equals 1 cup
2 cups	equals 1 pint
2 pints	equals 1 quart
4 quarts	equals 1 gallon
2 tablespoons	equals 1 fluid ounce
1 cup	equals 8 fluid ounces
16 ounces	equals 1 pound

Baked Chicken Maryland

GRITS CASSEROLE

4 c. boiling water
2 c. quick-cooking grits
1 t. salt

When grits are cooked, chop up:

1 roll garlic cheese
¼ lb. butter

Stir into grits and mix well until melted. Break 2 eggs into a cup and fill ½ full with the grits mixture, then stir into remainder of grits. Top with grated American cheese. Bake in a shallow, greased casserole for 45 minutes at 350°.

An old Southern recipe. It is a real winner at pot luck dinners. Try it with ham or chicken.

Frances Louise Dicks

HUSH PUPPIES

2 c. cornmeal
1 T. flour
1 t. baking powder
1 t. salt
½ t. baking soda
3 T. finely chopped onion (optional)
1 c. buttermilk
1 egg, beaten

Combine dry ingredients. Add onion, buttermilk and egg. Mix well. Drop by tablespoonfuls into deep hot fat (375°) and fry to a golden brown. Drain on absorbent paper. Serve very hot.

SOUTH CAROLINA SPOON BREAD
(As a Southerner makes it)

3 T. butter   ¼ c. cornmeal
3 eggs   1 t. salt
1 pt. milk

Heat milk in double boiler, stir in cornmeal and cook slowly until thick and smooth. Remove from heat and add butter and salt. Let cool while beating egg whites stiff. Beat egg yolks and add to cornmeal mixture, then fold in egg whites and bake for 30 minutes in a buttered pan in a 325 to 375° oven.

Alba M. Wahl

CORN BREAD

1 c. sifted flour
¾ c. yellow cornmeal
1 t. salt
1 T. baking powder
4 T. sugar
1 c. milk
2 eggs
¼ c. melted butter

Place first 5 ingredients in a mixing bowl. Then into a 2-cup measuring cup place remaining ingredients. Beat well with eggbeater. Add to dry ingredients all at once. Blend but do not beat. Pour into a well-greased 8-inch square pan. Bake at 400° for 30 minutes. Bread is done when a toothpick inserted in center comes out clean.

Eulalie Kinney

OLD SOUTH CRACKLING CAKES

3 c. cornmeal   ½ c. buttermilk
1 c. water   ⅛ t. salt
6 t. cracklings

Mix pork cracklings into meal with water and salt. Add buttermilk and stir well. Drop by spoonfuls until you have the desired size for individual cake onto heated greased griddle. Brown well on both sides. Serve with fresh vegetables.

Virginia K. Oliver

MAMA'S SOUTHERN DUMPLINGS

1 c. flour
1 t. baking powder
¼ t. powdered sage
½ t. salt
2½ T. shortening
3½ T. milk
2 T. chicken broth

Sift dry ingredients together. Cut in the shortening until mixture is finely blended. Add milk and broth, beating thoroughly. Roll out on a floured board till dough is very thin. Cut into narrow strips, and drop in a lattice-work pattern onto boiling chicken fricassee. Be sure to let the broth boil over each layer of dumplings so dough does not stick together. Cover tightly and simmer five minutes longer. Just before serving, garnish with chopped parsley or chives.

Andrew J. Shafer

PORCUPINE MEATBALLS

1 lb. ground meat (veal, beef and pork)
1 egg
   Chopped onion, browned in small
   amount of butter
¼ t. powdered sage
   Salt and pepper to taste
¼ c. uncooked rice which has been brought
   to a boil in either water or beef
   bouillon stock

Mix the above ingredients and form into balls. Arrange in a shallow casserole. Add 1 can of tomato soup and 1 can of water. Bake in a moderate oven until done.

These meatballs are delicious served with au gratin potatoes, Brussels sprouts and a fruit salad.

HAMBURGERS

I don't know when they first were made
Or just where they began,
But hamburgers just seem to me
So all-American.

They're served throughout our land today
In many different ways...
In roadside stands and sandwich shops,
In ball parks and cafes.

It's fun to dress them up a bit
With mayonnaise and cheese,
With pickles and tomatoes,
Or lettuce, if you please.

Sometimes you'll find them barbecued
Or char-broiled for a while,
Or served with salad and with fries
In California style.

However I may find them served,
They always seem to please...
I nominate the hamburger
For dining joy and ease!

Craig E. Sathoff

BROCCOLI BAKE

  2 pkgs. frozen broccoli
  1 can cream of mushroom soup, undiluted
½ c. mayonnaise
½ c. grated sharp cheese
  1 c. crushed cheese crackers
  1 T. lemon juice
  1 jar (2 oz.) pimiento, chopped
¼ c. slivered almonds

Cook and drain broccoli. Arrange broccoli in a buttered casserole. Mix soup, mayonnaise, lemon juice and cheese and spoon over broccoli. Top with pimiento, crackers and nuts. Bake at 350° for 20 to 30 minutes.

Juanita Patrick

PEANUT-RICE ROAST

1 c. peanut butter
1 c. (or more) water
1 medium onion, cut fine
1 t. sage or poultry seasoning
1 t. salt
2 c. cooked rice

Emulsify peanut butter with water until the consistency of thick cream. Add other ingredients and mix well. Bake at 350° for 45 minutes to 1 hour, or until firm.

Hazel M. Lee

HOMINY GRITS CASSEROLE

1½ c. hominy grits
  6 c. boiling water

Cook as directed.
Add:

  2 t. savory salt
  1 t. salt
½ c. margarine
½ lb. grated cheddar cheese
  3 eggs, well beaten
  3 dashes tabasco sauce

Pour into well-greased baking dish and bake at 250° for 1 hour. Serves 12.

Edith Goodrich Cox

SOUTHERN EGGPLANT

  1 medium-sized eggplant
  2 medium-sized onions, sliced
    (about 1 cup)
  2 T. butter
  3 tomatoes, peeled and cut into eighths or
    2 cups cooked tomatoes
1¼ t. salt
¼ t. white pepper
  1 7-oz. can shrimp, drained and cut
¼ c. bread crumbs, toasted and buttered

Cook eggplant, covered, in 1 inch boiling water until tender (about 25 minutes). Cool, peel and dice. Cook onion in butter until tender. Add tomatoes and cook until soft. Add seasonings, shrimp and eggplant and mix. Pour mixture into a greased 1½-quart casserole. Top with buttered crumbs. Bake, covered, in a preheated 350° oven about ½ hour.

PECAN PIE

1 c. dark Karo syrup
½ c. sugar
3 eggs
1 t. vanilla
¾ stick butter or margarine
¾ c. chopped pecans

Combine syrup, sugar and butter in a saucepan. Heat over medium heat until butter is melted. Add well beaten eggs and vanilla. After beating well, add ½ cup of pecans and mix, then pour into unbaked pie shell and sprinkle the rest of the pecans on top of the pie. Bake in 350° oven for about 45 minutes or until golden brown.

Mrs. Joseph B. Sellers

EASY COCONUT-CREAM PIE

1 5-oz. pkg. vanilla pudding and
   pie filling
3¼ c. milk
3 T. sugar
1 egg, slightly beaten
2 T. butter
1⅓ c. flaked coconut
1 baked 9-inch pie shell, cooled
   Whipped cream

Combine pie filling mix, milk, sugar and egg in saucepan. Blend well. Cook and stir over medium heat until mixture comes to a full boil. Remove from heat. Stir in butter and 1 cup of the coconut. Cool about 5 minutes, stirring once or twice.

Pour into pie shell. Cover surface with wax paper. Chill at least 3 hours. Remove paper and garnish with whipped cream. Sprinkle with remaining coconut.

Elizabeth Lou Sigler

PINEAPPLE CHIFFON PIE

1 No. 2 can crushed pineapple
1 c. granulated sugar
2 T. flour (heaping)
2 T. butter
3 egg yolks, beaten

Beat egg whites until stiff and set aside. Cream butter, sugar, and egg yolks and add flour. Add crushed pineapple and fold in egg whites. Put mixture in unbaked pie shell. Bake at 325° until crust is golden brown and filling is firm.

Mrs. Paul J. Clark

ORANGE BLOSSOMS

1 large pkg. yellow or lemon cake mix

Mix as directed on box and bake 8 to 10 minutes in a 350° oven in bite-size muffin tins. (The larger tins are not as good.) While hot, dunk in syrup on both sides and remove to wax paper to set.

SYRUP

Juice from 2 oranges
Juice from 2 lemons
Grated rind from 2 lemons
Grated rind from 2 oranges
1 lb. and 1 cup powdered sugar

Mix all the above together thoroughly. (I use the mixer on this first and let it stand while I mix the cake batter without washing the mixer.)

These may be frozen. One package makes between 85 and 110 cupcakes. I fill the tins about ½ full.

Rosalie L. Kennedy

ORANGE DATE CAKE

½ c. butter
1 c. sugar
2 eggs
1 medium unpeeled seedless orange,
   ground (about 1⅓ c.)
1 8-oz. pkg. dates, ground (about 1 c.)
2¼ c. sifted all-purpose flour
1 t. baking soda
¼ t. salt
1 c. dairy sour cream

TOPPING

1 c. dairy sour cream
2 T. sifted confectioners' sugar

Cream butter, gradually add sugar and beat until light and fluffy. Add eggs, then ground orange (including all juice) and dates. (At this time mixture may appear curdled.) Sift together flour, baking soda and salt. Add to creamed mixture alternately with sour cream, beginning and ending with dry ingredients. Turn into 9-inch square buttered pan. Bake 50 to 60 minutes at 350°. Cool on wire rack.

In a small bowl combine sour cream and confectioners' sugar. Spread over cake and serve while still warm.

PECAN FRUIT CAKE

1½ lb. pecan halves
1 pkg. seedless raisins
2 c. finely cut, candied orange peel
3 c. sifted flour
2 t. baking powder
½ t. salt
4 t. nutmeg
1 c. butter
1½ c. sugar
6 eggs, separated
1 c. bourbon whiskey

Cut each of the pecan halves into three crosswise slices. Rinse raisins in hot water, drain and dry on a towel. Mix pecans, raisins and orange peel with one cup of the flour. Sift the remaining 2 cups flour with the baking powder, salt and nutmeg. Cream butter and sugar, using a very large mixing bowl. Beat egg yolks until thickened and lemon colored. Beat into creamed mixture. Add sifted dry ingredients alternately with bourbon, mixing until smooth each time. Gradually fold in the pecan mixture. Beat egg whites stiff and fold in. Turn into greased 10-inch angel food cake pan lined with brown paper greased on both sides. Let stand 10 minutes. Bake in a 300° oven for about 3 hours or until cake tester inserted in center comes out clean. Place cake in pan on wire rack until partly cool. Turn out right side up. Cool completely. Leave brown paper on cake. Wrap tightly and store in refrigerator for a few days before slicing. Continue refrigerator storage as long as the cake lasts.

Mrs. Wade W. Fenton

DAINTY TEA CAKES

1 c. butter	½ t. baking powder
⅔ c. sugar	1 t. vanilla
1 egg	⅛ t. salt
2½ c. flour	

Cream butter and sugar. Add egg and mix well. Add all dry ingredients which have been mixed and sifted together. Add vanilla. Roll out and cut with cookie cutter. Bake at 400° for 10 to 12 minutes.

Mrs. John Ezzell

FRANKLIN NUT CAKE

1 lb. butter or margarine
2 c. sugar
6 eggs
½ lb. candied cherries
½ lb. candied pineapple
1 lb. pecans
4 c. cake flour
1 t. baking powder
¼ t. salt
2 t. vanilla

Cream butter and sugar; add beaten eggs. Sift 3 cups of flour with baking powder and salt. Add to mixture and mix well. Add remaining cup of flour to chopped fruit and nuts, then add to mixture. Add vanilla and mix well. Place in greased pan. Bake 3 hours at 250°. Test after 2½ hours.

Hazel N. Bullock

BOURBON BALLS

No baking, very good for the Christmas season.

1 6-oz. pkg. semisweet chocolate chips
3 T. white corn syrup
¼ c. bourbon
½ c. sugar
1¼ c. crushed vanilla wafers (about 35)
1 c. chopped pecans
1 container of chocolate sprinkles

Melt chocolate chips in top of double boiler or in pan over hot water. Remove from heat. Blend in corn syrup, sugar and bourbon. Stir in vanilla wafer crumbs and pecans.

Take one teaspoon of mixture at a time and roll between palms of hands. Keep hands cool with cold water and slightly greased with butter or margarine. Put sprinkles in small bowl and roll balls in sprinkles to coat well. Place on cookie sheet and chill for several hours.

Then pack in a pretty tin box, waxed paper on bottom and between layers. Keep in refrigerator until ready to serve.

Mrs. Paul Hartmann

GALA FRUIT-FILLED MELON

1 large watermelon
1 cantaloupe
1 lb. seedless grapes
3 oranges
1 ripe pineapple
1 qt. fresh strawberries, blueberries or other berries in season
¾ c. honey
¼ c. lemon juice
Fresh mint

Cut through the watermelon lengthwise, removing about one third. (Refrigerate this third for future use, wrapped in foil.) Scoop out the fruit from the larger melon section in large pieces, and scallop edge of watermelon as shown above to form the bowl for holding the fruit melange. Cut melon balls from the scooped-out fruit and from the cantaloupe. Prepare remaining fruit as for fruit cup, reserving some of the best berries with hulls on for garnish. Combine cut-up fruit in a large bowl and add the honey and lemon juice. (One-half cup kirsch, sherry or apricot brandy may be added if desired.) Chill the melon and the cut-up fruit separately, covered with foil. Fill shell with fruit and garnish with mint leaves.

SALTED PEANUT CAKE

An old cake recipe with a new flavor. Salted peanuts, a favorite snack food of all ages, may now be enjoyed in a cake. It's a very old recipe but now putting the peanuts in the electric blender grinds them to the consistency of fine flour, giving the cake a new and unusual flavor.

  1 c. granulated sugar
  ½ c. shortening
  1 egg
  1 c. sour milk (or add 2 T. vinegar to a cup of milk and let it stand 15 minutes before using)
  1 t. baking soda
1⅓ c. all-purpose flour
  1 c. ground salted peanuts (Spanish peanuts with jackets)

Cream shortening and sugar; add egg and mix well. The teaspoon of baking soda is added to the sour milk, which makes the sour milk light and bubbly. Add this cup of sour milk to the first mixture. Add the flour gradually and last stir in the ground salted peanuts. Bake in a greased 9 x 9-inch cake pan or round layer cake pan for 45 minutes in a preheated oven at 350°. Ice sparingly with white icing and sprinkle ground peanuts over the moist icing. A double recipe can make a two-layer cake.

Using the salted peanuts, no salt or vanilla is used. It is a moist cake with nutty toasted flavor.

Julia K. Sincak

KUMQUAT ICE CREAM

1 qt. whipping cream, scalded
2 c. sugar
4 eggs, separated
1 c. minced kumquats in syrup
1 T. curacao

Mix sugar and beaten egg yolks. Add cream slowly and cook, stirring constantly until slightly thickened. Remove from heat. Cool. Stir in remaining ingredients. Beat egg whites until stiff; fold into cream mixture. Freeze in refrigerator tray until firm.

SWEET POTATO CAKE

1½ c. cooking oil
  2 c. sugar
  4 eggs, separated
  4 T. hot water
2½ c. sifted cake flour
  3 t. baking powder
  ¼ t. salt
  1 t. ground cinnamon
  1 t. ground nutmeg
1½ c. grated raw sweet potatoes
  1 c. chopped nuts (black walnuts are good)
  1 t. vanilla

Combine cooking oil and sugar and beat until smooth. Add egg yolks and beat well. Add hot water, then dry ingredients which have been sifted together. Stir in potatoes, nuts and vanilla. Beat well. Beat egg whites until stiff and fold into mixture. Bake in three greased 8-inch layer cake pans at 350° for 25 to 30 minutes. Cool and frost with following frosting.

FROSTING FOR SWEET POTATO CAKE

1 large can evaporated milk
1 c. sugar
½ c. margarine
3 egg yolks
1 t. vanilla
1⅓ c. flaked coconut
1 c. pecans or black walnuts

Combine milk, sugar, margarine, egg yolks and vanilla in saucepan. Cook over medium heat about 12 minutes, stirring constantly, until mixture thickens. Remove from heat and add coconut and nuts. Beat until cool and spread on cake.

Norma Jean Clinton

Kumquat Ice Cream

PECAN CRUNCH COOKIES

1 c. butter or margarine
½ c. sugar
1 t. vanilla
1 c. finely crushed potato chips
½ c. chopped pecans
2½ T. ground pecans
2 c. all-purpose flour

Cream together butter, sugar and vanilla. Add crushed potato chips, chopped pecans and ground pecans. Stir in flour to make stiff dough. Form small balls using about 1 teaspoon dough for each. Press balls flat on ungreased cookie sheet, using a tumbler that has been dipped in sugar. Bake at 350° for 16 to 18 minutes or until very lightly browned.

Mary Cunnyngham

SWEET POTATO PUDDING

2 c. peeled and grated sweet potatoes
1 c. sugar
1 T. flour
½ c. melted butter
2 c. sweet milk
½ t. salt
1 t. nutmeg
½ t. cinnamon

Combine all ingredients and place in buttered baking dish. Bake in a 350° oven for 2 hours. Serve warm.

Margaret Welsh

SOUTHERN RICE PUDDING

2 c. cooked rice
Pinch of salt
1 can drained crushed pineapple
½ pt. cream, whipped

Mix together and spoon into serving dishes. Add dab of whipping cream to top along with red cherry for color if desired.

Lois J. Martinec

OLD-FASHIONED AMBROSIA

10 lbs. Florida oranges
1 can or bag flaked or shredded coconut
1½ c. pecans, quartered
1 small jar red maraschino cherries
1 small jar green maraschino cherries
(½ c. favorite bourbon or gin is optional)

Peel oranges and section and pit them. Retain juice. Add remaining ingredients, stir thoroughly and chill. Serve in small glass dishes.

This recipe serves 16 and usually is served with a favorite fruit cake.

Ambrosia gradually becomes discolored when it is chilled and should be eaten by the end of second day.

Mrs. C. E. Peverall

I love the stately southern mansions
   with their tall white columns;
They look through avenues of trees, over
   fields where the cotton is growing.
I can see the flutter of white frocks along
   their shady porches,
Music and laughter float from the windows,
   the yards are full of hounds and horses . . .
They have all ridden away, yet the houses
   have not forgotten;
They are proud of their name and place
   but their doors are always open,
For the thing they remember best is the
   pride of their ancient hospitality.

Author Unknown

NORTH CENTRAL

NORTH DAKOTA   WISCONSIN

SOUTH DAKOTA   ILLINOIS

NEBRASKA   MICHIGAN

MINNESOTA   INDIANA

IOWA   OHIO

FISH FILLETS IN A PACKAGE

1 lb. fish fillets, fresh or frozen
Salt and pepper
Paprika
1 small onion, sliced
1 or 2 very thinly sliced carrots
3 T. butter
½ c. tomato sauce
Lemon wedges

Thaw fillets, if frozen, until they can be cut easily. Divide fish into four portions. Prepare four 14-inch squares of Heavy Duty Reynolds Wrap. Roll or fold fish and arrange in center of each square. Sprinkle with seasonings and add remaining ingredients, except lemon wedges, dividing them equally. Bring Reynolds Wrap up over fish and seal. Place packages in a shallow pan and bake in a 400° oven for 25 minutes. Serve with lemon wedges.

FISH BOIL

6 medium-sized potatoes.(Do not peel, but cut a thin slice from each end.)
6 onions
1 c. salt
4 lbs. fresh fish steaks

In a large covered kettle, bring about 5 quarts of water to a boil. Add the potatoes, cover and boil gently for 20 minutes. Add onions and salt. Cover again and cook over medium heat for 15 minutes.

Then place a slotted tray over the potatoes and onions, or cover with a cheesecloth that extends over the sides of the kettle. This will make the removal of the fish much easier.

Now add the fish, cover and boil 12 minutes. To test, spear a potato and a fish steak. Do not overcook. The fish should be cooked only until it flakes easily with a fork.

Lift the fish to a serving tray and surround with the potatoes, onions and butter. Serve with coleslaw, beverage and pie for dessert. Serves 4 to 6.

BAKED FISH

1 4-lb. fish
2 c. soft bread crumbs
½ c. chopped green pepper
½ c. chopped celery
¼ c. chopped onion
¼ c. butter
¾ t. sage
Salt and pepper
½ c. hot water

Select a fresh lake trout, pike, whitefish or bass weighing about 4 pounds. Scale, clean and wash fish; drain well and dry with cloth.

Melt butter and slowly cook the onion, green pepper and celery, but do not brown. Pour over the bread crumbs, add seasonings and mix well.

Rub inside of fish with salt and melted butter. Place dressing in fish and sew or skewer together with toothpicks. Place in shallow buttered baking dish. Place dish in pan of hot water and bake in a 350° oven for 1¼ hours. Serve on hot platter garnished with wedges of lemon and parsley. Serve with tartar sauce.

Fish Fillets in a Package

SAUERKRAUT
(Recipe)

When August has come back again
And the cabbages are stout
And splitting in the summer sun...
It's time to make some kraut.

I like best the kraut-cutters
They used in years gone by...
A wooden frame with three sharp blades
To lower or raise high.

When cabbage has been cut up fine
And packed in quart jars tight,
Then add a teaspoonful of salt
And sugar...a pinch is right.

Then slowly fill the jars up full
With water, boiling hot,
And seal and store a month or two...
Then find your cooking pot!

Cook kraut with weiners or with ham
Or spareribs if you wish
Or Polish sausage or pork hocks
For good meals in one dish.

Craig E. Sathoff

STUFFED PORK CHOPS

Have pockets cut in 6 double loin pork chops.

    3 T. butter
    1 t. minced onion
    ¼ c. finely sliced mushrooms
    ½ c. crumbled American blue cheese
    ¾ c. fine dry bread crumbs
       Dash of salt

Melt butter in skillet. Add onion and mushrooms. Cook 5 minutes. Remove from heat and stir in blue cheese, bread crumbs and salt. Stuff pockets in each chop with dressing. Secure with picks. Bake at 325° for 1 hour or until done.

SAUERKRAUT SALAD

    1 can (1 lb. 12 oz.) sauerkraut
    ½ t. celery seed
    1 green pepper, chopped
    1 c. celery, chopped
    1½ c. sugar
    ½ c. vinegar
    ¾ t. salt
    1 small can pimiento
    ½ c. salad oil
    ½ c. water
       Green onion, if desired

Combine all ingredients and let stand 24 hours before serving. Keeps for weeks in refrigerator.

Elsie Auer

MILWAUKEE GRILLED DINNER

    4 smoked loin pork chops,
       cut ½ to ¾ inch thick
    1 12-oz. can whole kernel corn
    2 large cooked potatoes, cut into halves
       Melted butter
       Paprika
    4 canned pear halves
    4 t. cranberry-orange relish

Score fat edge of chops; place on broiler rack. Pour the corn and liquid into the broiler pan; cover with rack on which chops have been placed. Place about 4 inches below burner and broil about 10 minutes. Turn chops; add potatoes, brush with melted butter and sprinkle with paprika; broil about 5 minutes. Arrange cranberry-filled pear halves on rack. Broil about 5 minutes longer.

GERMAN POTATO SALAD

9 potatoes	2 t. salt
6 slices bacon	½ t. celery seed
¾ c. chopped onion	Dash of pepper
2 T. flour	¾ c. water
2 T. sugar	¼ c. vinegar

Cook potatoes. Set aside to cool. In a large skillet, fry bacon until crisp. Remove bacon and drain. Over low heat, stir onion in bacon drippings until brown. Blend in flour, sugar, salt, celery seed and pepper. Cook until mixture is thick and bubbly. Remove from heat. Stir in vinegar and water. Heat and boil for 1 minute. Slice potatoes thin and add to mixture and heat until potatoes are coated. Add bacon and stir gently.

Gladys Hilpertshauser

CUBED BEEF SAUERBRATEN

2 lbs. beef chuck, cut in cubes
Butter or margarine
1 c. vinegar
3 c. water
2 T. sugar
2 small onions—cut in small pieces
Small bag of pickle spices
12 gingersnaps, crumbled

Brown beef in a small amount of butter or margarine and combine with remaining ingredients except gingersnaps. Cook slowly for about 2 hours or until meat is tender. Add gingersnaps and stir until gravy thickens. Let meat stand for a while until flavors are well blended. Serve over boiled noodles. Leftover beef may be used. This reduces cooking time to about 1 hour.

Vera Hardman

SOUTHERN ILLINOIS HOMINY

2½ c. or 1 large can white or yellow hominy
6 to 8 slices of bacon
5 eggs
½ t. salt
⅛ t. oregano
Sprinkle of pepper

Fry bacon in large skillet till crisp, remove bacon. Pour bacon drippings off, reserving 2½ tablespoons in skillet. Pour hominy in skillet and stir until lightly browned. Crumble the bacon and set it aside.

Beat together eggs, salt, pepper and oregano. Pour over hominy in the skillet. Stir often, cooking until eggs are set, just a few minutes. Before serving, sprinkle the crumbled bacon over the hominy. Serve with a green salad, hot biscuits and butter.

Golde Hoover

ROYAL FEAST
SOUTHERN ILLINOIS HOMINY

Iceberg White or Golden Morn,
Hominy is the king of corn,
Born with the blossoms of wind-soft May
To wave in the warmth of a summer day;
Tasseling tall with the August heat
When berries hang ripened, sugar-sweet.
Dry husks rattle when wild geese call,
To blend with the reds and golds of fall.
Garnered with frost, homemade or canned,
When a tiptop tempting treat is planned.
Though the day is dark and snowflakes fly,
Your serving is summer and a deep blue sky.

Dan A. Hoover

CHIPPEWA INDIAN
FRIED BREAD

4 c. flour	**2 t. salt**
3 T. baking powder	**1 T. shortening**
2 T. dry milk	**2 c. warm water**

Sift dry ingredients together and mix in shortening. Gradually add the warm water. Mix gently and knead until dough is soft to handle. Cover and let dough rise, about 20 minutes. Roll into golf-size balls, flatten with hands and make hole in center (will look like doughnuts). Drop in hot vegetable oil approximately ¾-inch deep. Turn when golden brown. Serve immediately with butter and jam.

Note: Also delicious to make a taco meat, cheese, lettuce mixture and serve over bread that is rolled ¼-inch thick (about size of salad plate) and then fried.

Constance M. Simenson

FARM PUDDING

4 or 5 slices dry, stale, white bread
2 c. applesauce, sweetened to taste
¼ t. cinnamon
¼ t. nutmeg
2 T. butter
2 c. milk
2 eggs, beaten
½ c. sugar
    Salt to taste
1 t. vanilla extract

Prepare bread crumbs by breaking into small pieces. Put half in bottom of a buttered deep baking dish (1½ qt.). Add cinnamon and nutmeg to applesauce and spread over the bread in dish. Cover with remaining bread pieces. Dot with butter. Mix milk, eggs, sugar, salt and vanilla and pour over the bread and applesauce. Bake at about 350° for 1 hour or until pudding is puffed and set. Serve with half-and-half cream while still warm, or serve cold with a dollop of whipped sweet cream or a scoop of vanilla ice cream. Serves 6 to 8.

Zelda M. Masten

PERSIMMON PUDDING

1 c. flour
½ t. salt
1 t. baking soda
½ t. cinnamon
½ c. walnuts
½ c. dates, cut up
3 T. melted shortening
¾ c. sugar
1 egg
½ c. milk
1 c. ripe persimmon pulp

Sift together the flour, salt, soda and cinnamon. Mix egg and sugar thoroughly, then add persimmon pulp which has been pressed through a coarse sieve. Mix again. Add shortening, nuts and dates. Fold in flour mixture and milk. Blend until smooth. Fill greased molds three-quarters full and bake at 300° for 1 hour. (If made in small muffin tins, baking time will be shorter.) Serve with hard sauce or ice cream. Best served warm. If they have been stored in freezer, remove and thaw. Wrap in foil and heat in the oven.

Emma Dredla

GRAHAM CRACKER PUDDING

1 envelope unflavored gelatin
¾ c. cold water
4 eggs, separated
1 c. sugar
⅔ c. pineapple juice
1 c. whipping cream
20 graham crackers, rolled into fine crumbs
½ c. melted butter

Dissolve gelatin in the cold water and set aside. Beat egg yolks and add ½ c. sugar and the pineapple juice. Cook in double boiler, stirring constantly, until thickened. Remove from stove and add the dissolved gelatin. Cool, stirring occasionally. Beat 4 egg whites until they hold soft peaks, then gradually add the ½ c. sugar, beating constantly. Fold into mixture. Add the cream which has been whipped.

Combine graham cracker crumbs and melted butter. Put half the crumb mixture in bottom of an 8 x 12-inch baking dish. Pour pudding over the crumbs, then sprinkle remaining crumbs over the top. Chill thoroughly.

Mrs. John Waite

TRANSPLANTING

We left New England many years ago
And came to live and build on Midwest land;
I planted lilacs in a hedge below
The shed; they blossomed purple against sand.

I brought my braided mats and pewter ware,
A Pilgrim warming pan and featherbed,
My highboy, Sandwich glass and Winthrop chair,
My recipes for succotash and bread.

I had baked beans for supper Saturday,
And put white shells about the garden walk;
We never lost our clipped New England way
Of answering direct to neighbors' talk.

Here in the sandy country, I remember woods
Of lady's slippers, sweeter than this sage;
New England isn't place or neighborhood . . .
It's part of coursing blood and heritage.

E. Harriet Donlevy

STRAWBERRY SHORTCAKE

- 4 c. flour
- ½ c. sugar
- 2 T. plus 2 t. baking powder
- 1 t. salt
- ¾ c. butter
- 4 eggs
- ½ c. milk
- ¼ c. soft butter
- 2 qts. strawberries, stemmed and sliced
- 2 c. sugar (approx.)
- 2 c. heavy cream
- ¼ c. sugar
- 2 t. vanilla

Into a mixing bowl sift the flour, ½ cup sugar, baking powder and salt. Cut or rub in ¾ cup butter until particles are fine. Beat eggs with milk, add dry ingredients and mix thoroughly to make a soft dough. Turn out onto lightly floured board and pat into a thick circle to fit bottom of a buttered Dutch oven, heavy casserole or frying pan. Bake in a 375° oven for 40 minutes or until golden brown. Place on wire rack to cool.

Split into three layers; spread each with soft butter. Meantime gently mix strawberries with sugar to sweeten. Chill for 30 minutes. Whip cream with ¼ cup sugar and vanilla. To assemble, place bottom shortcake layer on serving platter. Top with one-third of the berries and spoon on one-third of the cream. Top with the second shortcake layer. Repeat layering of berries and cream; repeat with third layer. Cut into deep wedges. Makes 10 servings.

Barb Maybee

CREAM PIE WITH CHERRY GLAZE

1 baked 9-inch pie shell
¾ c. sugar
⅓ c. all-purpose flour
¼ t. salt
2 c. milk
3 egg yolks, slightly beaten
3 T. butter
1 t. vanilla
1 can (1 lb.) red tart pitted cherries in heavy syrup, drained
½ c. cherry syrup
½ c. sugar
2 T. cornstarch
1 T. butter

In a large saucepan combine sugar, flour and salt; gradually add milk. Cook over medium heat, stirring constantly, until thickened. Cook 2 additional minutes. Blend a small amount of hot mixture into egg yolks; return all to pan. Cook 1 minute. (Do not boil.) Remove from heat; add butter and vanilla. Cool to lukewarm, stirring occasionally. Pour into pie shell. Cool on wire rack.

Meanwhile, in a 1½-quart saucepan combine syrup, sugar and cornstarch. Add cherries. Cook over medium heat, stirring constantly, until thickened. Cook 2 additional minutes. Remove from heat; stir in butter. If desired, add a few drops red food coloring. Cool. Spread glaze over pie. Chill.

FRESH BLUEBERRY PIE

4 c. fresh blueberries
1 9-inch baked piecrust
1 c. sugar
3 T. cornstarch
¼ t. salt
¼ c. water

Line baked piecrust with 2 cups fresh blueberries. Cook together the remaining blueberries and other ingredients until thick, stirring constantly. Remove from heat. Add 1 tablespoon butter. Cool. Pour over blueberries in piecrust. Serve with whipped cream or ice cream.

Mrs. L. P. Bora

FRENCH SILK PIE

1 baked 9-inch pie shell
½ c. butter
1¼ c. powdered sugar
1½ sq. chocolate
1 t. vanilla
2 eggs

Cream butter and add sugar gradually, creaming well. Blend in melted and cooled chocolate, then vanilla. Add 1 egg at a time, beating 5 minutes after each addition.

Turn into pie shell. Chill 1 to 2 hours. May be topped with whipped cream and garnished with nuts.

Grace Rosser

HARRISON CREAM PIE

Blend:

1½ c. sugar
⅓ c. flour
2½ c. light cream

Add:

½ t. salt
2 t. vanilla
1 T. melted butter

Pour filling into an unbaked 9-inch pie shell.

Bake 10 minutes at 450°. Reduce heat to 325° and bake another 25 minutes.

Harrison Pie is supposed to be one of the first soft pies to be served by Indiana's gourmet cooks. Legend tells us that the pie was first served around the turn of the century by Mrs. Harrison, wife of Indiana's Governor Benjamin Harrison.

Esther Perry

CHERRY PICKING TIME

It's cherry-picking time again
And, oh, what joy it is
To see the ripened fruit hang low,
The bright red fruit, sun-kissed.

Short days ago white blossoms sweet
Bedecked the orchard trees,
And gathering nectar from each bloom
Were neighboring honeybees.

The blossoms now have turned to fruit,
The harvesttime is nigh;
How tasty will these pickings be
In Cherry-O-Cream Cheese Pie!

★ ★ ★

CHERRY-O-CREAM CHEESE PIE

1 8-oz. pkg. cream cheese
1 14-oz. can sweetened condensed milk
⅓ c. reconstituted lemon juice
1 t. vanilla
1 can prepared cherry pie filling
1 9-inch graham cracker crust

Combine cheese and condensed milk and beat until well blended (approximately 5 minutes at medium speed with electric mixer). Add juice and vanilla and mix until thick and creamy smooth.

Pour into one prepared 9-inch graham cracker crust and place in the refrigerator until chilled (about ½ hour). Top with cherry pie filling.

This makes a very fancy and pleasing dessert for any occasion.

Loise Pinkerton Fritz

RHUBARB CUSTARD PIE

6 c. cut up rhubarb   4 T. flour
3 c. sugar   Juice of 1 lemon
3 eggs

Mix together the above ingredients. Sprinkle a little flour on bottom of 2 ten-inch unbaked pie shells. Fill with rhubarb mixture and if desired add a lattice top. Bake at 450° for 10 minutes. Reduce heat and bake at 350° until knife inserted in pie comes out clean. Cool.

Mrs. Harold R. Kelly

EGG CUSTARD PIE

5 c. milk
¾ c. sugar
1 t. vanilla
½ t. almond extract
¼ t. salt
6 eggs, slightly beaten
1 unbaked pie shell, 11 to 12 inches, or 2 smaller pie shells

Scald milk; add sugar, flavorings and salt and mix together. Stir slowly into beaten eggs. Pour into unbaked pie shell; bake in 400° oven for 20 to 25 minutes.

Mrs. Paul E. King

CORN RELISH

½ c. flour
1 T. turmeric
¼ c. dry mustard
6 c. corn, cut from cob
2 red peppers, chopped
1 c. chopped cabbage
4 onions, chopped
1 qt. vinegar
2 T. salt
2 c. sugar
1½ T. celery seed

Blend flour, turmeric and mustard to a paste with a little of the vinegar. Mix all ingredients and simmer for 45 minutes, stirring frequently to prevent scorching. Seal in clean, hot jars. Makes 4 pints.

Mrs. Lawrence Latour

RHUBARB JAM

4 c. rhubarb, which has been cut in ½-inch pieces
4 c. sugar

Place in kettle and cook over very low heat until sugar is dissolved. Increase heat and cook until rhubarb is tender. Remove from heat, add one 3-oz. pkg. strawberry gelatin and stir until gelatin is dissolved. Pour into sterilized jars and seal.

Juanita Patrick

APPLE CAKE

1¼ c. sifted flour
  1 t. baking powder
 ½ t. salt
  1 t. sugar
 ½ c. butter
  1 egg yolk, beaten
  2 T. milk
 ¾ qt. sliced apples

Mix and sift flour, baking powder, salt and sugar. Cream butter, add sifted dry ingredients and mix. Combine egg yolk and milk and add to butter mixture. Mix. Press mixture on bottom of a buttered pan, 8 x 8 inches. Overlap apple slices into dough. Sprinkle with topping. Bake in preheated 375° oven about 50 minutes.

TOPPING

¾ c. sugar   ¼ t. cinnamon
1½ T. flour   2 T. butter

Mix sugar, flour and cinnamon; cut in butter until coarse.

BUTTERMILK POUND CAKE

1 c. butter
3 c. sugar
5 eggs, separated
1 c. buttermilk
⅓ t. baking soda, dissolved in buttermilk
3 c. flour
1 t. vanilla

Cream butter and sugar together; add beaten egg yolks. Add flour and milk and beat on medium speed. (High speed for portable mixers.) Fold in well-beaten egg whites and vanilla.

Bake in a greased tube pan for one hour and ten minutes at 325°.

Sue Harenchar

AUNT BERTHA'S INDIANA PERSIMMON PUDDING

1 qt. small persimmons, sieved to produce 2 c. pulp.
3 c. milk (2½ c. if large cultivated persimmons are used)
3 eggs
2 c. sugar
2 t. baking soda
2 c. flour
1 t. baking powder
1 t. cinnamon
1 t. nutmeg
½ t. salt
½ t. vanilla
1 T. melted butter

Combine persimmons with milk, which should be at room temperature. Add beaten eggs. Sift all dry ingredients together and gradually add dry ingredients and liquid together. Add vanilla and melted shortening last.

Pour into a large buttered glass baking dish or two 8 x 8-inch dishes. Bake at 350° for 1 hour or until knife comes out clean. Serve with whipped cream, ice cream or vanilla sauce. Serves 12 to 14. You may cut recipe in half. Serve warm or cool.

Mrs. Donald L. Jacobs

CRUMB CAKE

2 c. brown sugar
2½ c. flour
1 t. cinnamon, scant
½ c. butter

Mix with dough blender. Take out half cup for topping, then add to balance:

1 c. sour milk
1 t. soda
2 eggs

Mix and place in greased pan. Sprinkle the ½ cup reserved mixture on top. Add chopped nutmeats and chocolate chips, if desired, on top. Bake in a 350° oven.

Lucile Heck

BLUEBERRY CHEESE SLICES

BOTTOM LAYER

⅓ c. butter
⅓ c. brown sugar
1 c. flour
½ c. finely chopped walnuts
Pinch of salt

Mix ingredients and set aside ¾ c. of mixture. Press remainder into an 8 x 8-inch pan and bake at 350° for 12 minutes. Cool.

TOP LAYER

1 8-oz. pkg. cream cheese, softened
½ c. granulated sugar
1 egg
2 T. milk
1 T. lemon juice

Mix thoroughly.

Spread baked crumb layer with blueberry or any other favourite jam to about ⅓ of an inch. Spread with cheese mixture and finally sprinkle with reserved ¾ c. crumbs. Bake at 350° for 25 minutes. Slice when cool.

If using a glass baking dish, bake at cooler temperature.

Ella L. Katzberg

TASSIES

½ c. margarine
1 3-oz. pkg. cream cheese
1 c. flour

Mix together with spoon.

FILLING

Beat 1 egg.

Add:

¾ c. brown sugar
1 t. vanilla
1 T. melted butter
½ c. chopped nuts

Divide dough into 24 small balls and line very small muffin pans.

Add filling and bake 15 to 18 minutes at 350°, then 10 minutes at 250°.

Mrs. R. H. Alexander

PERSIMMON COOKIES

Blend together the following:

1 c. sugar
½ c. dark brown sugar
¾ c. butter or margarine
2 eggs
¾ c. persimmon pulp
1 t. vanilla

Sift together the following:

3 c. flour
1½ t. baking powder
1½ t. baking soda
1½ t. cinnamon
1 t. nutmeg
½ t. cloves
½ t. salt

Mix dry and wet ingredients and add:

1½ c. chopped walnuts
1½ c. raisins

Drop by teaspoon on ungreased cookie sheet and bake 20 minutes in 350° oven. Makes about 80 cookies.

Beatrice R. Cochrun

GOLDEN CHERRY CHEWS

¾ c. butter
2 c. cottage cheese
2¼ c. all-purpose flour
½ t. salt

Cream butter and cheese until fairly smooth; add flour and salt. (Add the last 1¼ cups flour by hand.) Chill several hours.

FILLING

1 can (1 lb.) red tart pitted cherries in water pack
½ c. sugar
2 T. cornstarch
½ t. almond extract
Confectioners' sugar

Drain cherries, reserving ¾ cup liquid. Combine sugar and cornstarch and gradually stir in liquid. Cook, stirring constantly, until thickened. Cook 2 more minutes. Add almond extract and cherries; cool. On a floured board roll ⅓ of dough to a 15 x 9-inch rectangle and ⅛-inch thickness. Cut into 3-inch squares. Place 2 cherries with sauce on each. Fold corners into center, pressing outer edges of square to flatten. Repeat with remaining dough. Bake 20 to 35 minutes at 375° on a buttered baking sheet. Cool on wire rack. Sprinkle with sugar.

OATMEAL COOKIES

1 c. flour
½ t. salt
½ t. baking powder
½ t. baking soda
½ c. each brown sugar and white sugar (or 1 c. brown sugar)
½ c. cooking oil
1 egg
1 T. water
1 t. vanilla
1½ c. uncooked oatmeal

Mix all dry ingredients, make a well and add the oil, egg, water and vanilla. Mix well. Drop from a teaspoon onto ungreased cookie sheet and flatten with a fork. Bake for 10 minutes at 350°.

Mrs. Amos J. C. Baldwin

ONION SOUP LOUISIANA STYLE

5 T. butter, divided
6 medium onions, sliced
1 qt. water
5 bouillon cubes
¾ t. tabasco, divided
6 slices French bread, toasted
2 T. grated parmesan cheese

Melt 4 tablespoons of the butter in a deep kettle. Add onions and cook until tender but not brown, stirring occasionally. Add water, bouillon cubes and ½ teaspoon of the tabasco sauce. Bring to a boil. Cover; reduce heat and simmer 30 minutes. When ready to serve, blend together the remaining 1 tablespoon butter with remaining ¼ teaspoon tabasco. Toast bread slices on one side under broiler. Spread untoasted side with tabasco butter and sprinkle with parmesan cheese. Place under broiler about 1 minute, until cheese is bubbly. Pour soup into a tureen or individual soup bowls. Float bread slices on top.

KANSAS

MISSOURI   LOUISIANA

ARKANSAS   OKLAHOMA

MISSISSIPPI   TEXAS

CHICKEN SOUP NEW ORLEANS

1 c. diced cooked ham
½ c. chopped onion
⅛ t. thyme
  Generous dash poultry seasoning
1 T. butter
3 cans (10½-oz. each) condensed chicken gumbo soup
3 soup cans water
1 c. cubed cooked chicken
1 pkg. (10-oz.) frozen asparagus cuts, cooked and drained

In a large kettle, brown ham and cook onion with seasonings in butter until tender. Add remaining ingredients. Heat and serve.

SHRIMP LOUISIANE CASSEROLE

1 c. chopped onions
¾ c. chopped green pepper
1 clove garlic, minced
2 T. butter or margarine
1 lb. peeled, deveined raw shrimp
1 10¾-oz. can condensed cream of mushroom soup*
3 c. cooked rice
1 T. chopped parsley
1½ T. lemon juice
1½ t. salt
¼ t. each black pepper and red pepper
2 slices white bread
½ c. milk

Sauté onions, green pepper and garlic in butter until tender crisp. Add shrimp and continue cooking 3 minutes longer. Stir in soup, rice, parsley, lemon juice and seasonings. Add bread which has been soaked in milk; mix well. Spoon into a buttered shallow 2-quart casserole. Sprinkle with paprika. Bake at 350° for 30 minutes. Makes 6 servings.

*Condensed cream of celery soup, condensed cream of chicken soup or condensed tomato soup may be substituted.

STUFFED FRANKFURTERS

2 T. minced onion
1 T. butter
1½ c. soft bread
 crumbs
¼ t. salt

⅛ t. pepper
8 frankfurters
8 strips bacon
Toothpicks

Sauté the onion in the butter about 3 minutes. Add the bread crumbs, salt and pepper, and mix thoroughly. Split frankfurters lengthwise. Fill with stuffing mixture. Wrap each frankfurter with a strip of bacon and secure at both ends with toothpicks. Place the stuffed frankfurters on broiler rack and broil 8 to 15 minutes turning them until bacon is well browned.

JAMBALAYA

1 T. butter or margarine
1 lb. ham, pork sausage or chicken or a combination of any of these meats
½ c. green pepper, chopped
1 clove garlic, minced
1 T. flour
3 c. canned tomatoes, diced
3 c. cooked shrimp
2 c. water
2 c. uncooked rice (long grain)
¼ t. oregano
½ t. thyme
½ t. basil
1 t. salt
⅛ t. red pepper
3 T. chopped parsley

Melt butter, add meat and green pepper. Cook for 3 minutes. Add flour and cook 2 minutes. Then add the tomatoes, shrimp, water, onion and let come to a boil. Add the rice and remaining ingredients, except the parsley. Cover and simmer until rice is tender and liquid is absorbed. Serve with parsley sprinkled on top.

NEW ORLEANS POOR BOY SANDWICH

1 15-oz. can roast beef and gravy (Leftover roast beef and gravy may be used)
1 t. yellow mustard
4 T. pickle relish
¼ t. Worcestershire sauce
French or Italian bread
Mayonnaise
Shredded lettuce
1 tomato, thinly sliced

Place roast beef and gravy in saucepan. Add mustard, pickle relish and Worcestershire sauce and heat thoroughly. Cut roll or bread lengthwise and spread with mayonnaise. Arrange beef slices on roll and cover with gravy, shredded lettuce and tomato slices.

CHILI DIP

1 c. cottage cheese
1 hard-cooked egg, finely chopped
1½ t. grated onion
1 t. chili powder
½ t. salt
3 T. pickle relish
1 T. stuffed olives, chopped

In a mixing bowl beat together cottage cheese, egg, onion, chili powder and salt until fairly smooth. Add pickle relish and olives; beat until blended. Cover and chill.

BARBECUE SAUCE FOR CHICKEN OR SPARERIBS

2 T. butter
1 c. catsup
½ c. chili sauce
1 t. dry mustard
Dash of tabasco
⅓ c. vinegar (scant)
2 t. Worcestershire sauce
2 T. brown sugar
Grated onion

Bring to boil before serving over meat.

Lorraine Raabe

SEAFOOD SUPREME

2 T. chopped onion
2 T. chopped green pepper
⅓ c. sliced celery
1 c. cooked rice
½ c. raw shrimp, peeled, deveined and chopped
½ c. crab meat, drained and flaked
⅓ c. mayonnaise
½ t. Worcestershire sauce
½ t. lemon juice
½ t. salt
⅛ t. pepper
¼ c. buttered soft bread crumbs

Combine all ingredients except bread crumbs. Mix well. Turn into a buttered shallow 1-quart casserole or individual seashells. Top with bread crumbs. Sprinkle with paprika if desired. Bake at 375° for 25 minutes.

NEW ORLEANS STUFFED BAKED FILLETS CREOLE

4 T. butter
2 T. chopped onion
4 T. chopped celery
2 T. chopped green pepper
2 T. flour
½ c. milk
½ c. fine dry bread crumbs
Pinch each of dried thyme, rosemary, and marjoram
1 c. cooked crab meat
1 c. cooked shrimp, cut in pieces
½ c. chopped parsley
¼ t. salt
Dash of pepper
1½ t. Worcestershire sauce
4 to 8 fillets of sole

Melt butter in saucepan. Stir in onion, celery and green pepper and cook until tender. Stir in flour, keeping mixture as smooth as possible. Add milk and cook until thickened. Remove from heat and stir in all remaining ingredients, except the fillets. Make a mound of the filling on each of the fillets, roll up ends and secure with a toothpick. Place in a shallow baking pan leaving space between fillets. Brush with melted butter, sprinkle with salt and paprika. Bake in preheated 350° oven for 15 minutes, then pour sauce over the fish, reduce heat to 325° and bake 30 minutes longer.

Charlene Myers

OKRA

Place 1½ pints frozen okra in a saucepan with ½ cup water. Add ½ teaspoon salt. Bring water quickly to boil, reduce heat and cook approximately 10 minutes until tender. Drain add 2 tablespoons butter, and serve hot.

CREOLE SAUCE

2 c. diced onions
2 c. diced celery
4 cloves garlic
2 c. chopped green peppers
4 T. olive oil
3 lbs. canned tomatoes, crushed
1 c. water
2 bay leaves
¼ t. thyme
4 T. chopped parsley
Salt and pepper to taste
1 T. cornstarch

Sauté onion, celery, garlic and peppers in olive oil. Add tomatoes, water and all other ingredients except cornstarch and simmer about one hour. Thicken with cornstarch.

Pass another dish of the sauce at the table to serve with the rice.

Charlene Myers

LOUISIANA BOILED RICE

Wash 1¼ cups long-grained rice thoroughly in cold water. Bring a large quantity of salted water to a hard boil in deep pot. Add the rice slowly so the boiling is not stopped. Scrape up grains that may have stuck to the bottom, and then do not touch them again until rice is done. Boil briskly, uncovered, for 17 minutes. Drain into a large colander and let cold water run through the grains for half a minute. Drain again, cover the colander and put in the oven long enough to reheat.

Charlene Myers

For an authentic Creole fish dinner, prepare New Orleans Stuffed Baked Fillets Creole, Louisiana Boiled Rice and Creole Sauce. Turn the rice out onto the middle of a large platter and drizzle with sauce. Arrange the stuffed fish around the rice on the platter. Pass another dish of sauce at the table.

MEXICAN MEAL

1 lb. lean ground beef
1 c. chopped onions
1 c. chopped green peppers
1 clove garlic, crushed
1 T. chili powder
1 t. salt
3 c. cooked rice
1 8-oz. can tomato sauce
¾ c. buttermilk
1 c. cubed cheddar cheese

Sauté beef, onions, green peppers, garlic and seasonings until meat and vegetables are tender but not brown. Stir in rice, tomato sauce and buttermilk; heat thoroughly. Fold in cheese. Serve with fresh green onions and corn chips if desired. Makes 6 servings.

Mexican Meal

BAYOU SHRIMP AND RICE

2 4½-oz. cans whole shrimp
4 T. butter
1 large onion, chopped
½ green pepper, sliced
1 12-oz. can peeled tomatoes
¼ t. garlic powder
½ t. salt
3 c. cooked rice

Drain shrimp. Cover with ice water and let stand 5 minutes. Drain again. In a saucepan melt butter or margarine and sauté onions and green peppers. Add tomatoes with liquid and all other seasonings; heat. Add shrimp; heat thoroughly and serve with hot rice.

CORN PUDDING

2 eggs	2 T. butter
1½ c. canned corn	1 c. milk
2 T. flour	⅛ t. pepper
2 T. sugar	½ t. salt

Beat eggs, add all other ingredients. Pour into greased casserole dish and bake 1 hour and 20 minutes, or until golden brown, at 350°.

Place casserole dish in pan of water to prevent burning.

Lillie Mae Kelly

Corn Pudding

Photo courtesy General Foods Corporation

MEX-TEX TOSTADOS

BEEF MIXTURE

¾ lb. ground beef
½ c. chopped onion
¼ c. shortening
3 cans (about 16 oz. each) red kidney beans
1 c. Open Pit Barbecue Sauce
¼ t. salt

Brown beef and onion in shortening. Add beans, 1 cup barbecue sauce and the salt. Simmer about 20 to 25 minutes. Meanwhile, make sauce:

SAUCE

1 c. Open Pit Barbecue Sauce
1 c. canned tomato puree
1 T. butter
1 to 2 t. chili powder

Combine 1 cup barbecue sauce, the tomato puree, butter, and chili powder. Simmer, uncovered, for 20 to 25 minutes.

12 frozen or canned tortillas
    Shredded lettuce, chopped onion,
    chopped tomatoes, grated cheese

Brown tortillas as directed on package. Spread each tortilla with ⅓ cup beef mixture. Pass bowls of shredded lettuce, onion, tomatoes, cheese and the sauce so that each person may top his tortilla to his liking. Makes 12 tostados or 6 servings.

BARBECUED SPARERIBS

Mix:

1 onion, diced
1 c. catsup or more (enough to make 2 cups when sauce is ready)
2 T. white vinegar
¼ t. red pepper
¼ t. chili powder
1 T. Worcestershire sauce
1 clove garlic, minced

Boil sauce 5 minutes. Makes enough sauce for 2 racks of ribs.

Start heating oven at 325°. Place spareribs in shallow open pan, cover with foil and roast ½ hour. Pour off fat, turn and roast ½ hour longer. Pour off fat again.

Cover ribs with sauce—increase oven heat to 400°. Roast spareribs uncovered, basting often, 45 minutes or until fork tender, very brown and glazed. Cut into pieces and serve.

Mrs. D. J. Liston

ARROZ CON POLLO

2½ lbs. choice chicken pieces
2½ T. butter or margarine
2 small cloves garlic, crushed
2 t. salt
⅛ t. pepper
⅛ t. paprika
3 slices bacon, finely diced
¼ c. each chopped onion and green pepper
1 c. uncooked rice
2 c. boiling chicken broth
½ c. canned tomatoes, crushed
   Pinch of saffron, optional
½ c. cooked green peas

Place chicken in baking dish, skin side up. Combine butter, 1 clove garlic, 1 teaspoon salt, pepper and paprika. Brush on chicken. Bake at 350° for 45 to 55 minutes or until golden brown. In oven-proof skillet, sauté bacon until lightly browned. Add onion, green pepper and remaining garlic. Cook until vegetables are tender. Do not brown. Add rice and cook for 2 minutes. Stir in chicken broth, tomatoes, saffron and remaining salt. Cover tightly and bake at 350° for 45 minutes or until rice is tender and liquid is absorbed. Add green peas and fluff lightly with a fork. Arrange cooked chicken over rice. Serves 6.

ROLL-UPS

FILLING

1 lb. ground chuck
1 large Bermuda onion, chopped
1 t. garlic salt
¼ t. pepper
1½ c. boiling water
2 t. vinegar
½ t. oregano
½ t. cumin

Combine all filling ingredients except water. Cook until browned. Add water and heat to boiling. Strain liquid into a bowl and skim off fat. Combine the liquid with tomato sauce and simmer 10 minutes.

PANCAKES

3 eggs
6 T. cornmeal
7 T. water
Dash of salt and pepper

Combine pancake ingredients and mix well. Use a vegetable spray on a small skillet and put on moderate heat. When pan is hot add about 2 tablespoons of batter, turning pan to coat evenly. When pancake is set reverse onto plate. Continue until all batter is used. Makes 12 pancakes.

TOPPING

2 c. seasoned tomato sauce (Spanish style)
3 oz. sharp cheddar cheese

Preheat oven to 300°. Fill pancakes with meat, place in shallow oven-proof pan, and top with sauce and cheese. Heat until cheese melts.

Patricia Mason

CREOLE CORN

1 onion, chopped
2 T. butter or margarine
2½ c. tomatoes, peeled and chopped
1 t. sugar
1 t. salt
¼ t. pepper
2 c. whole kernel corn
½ green pepper, chopped

Cook onion in butter until lightly browned. Add tomatoes, sugar, seasonings and corn. Simmer 10 minutes. Add green pepper and simmer 5 minutes longer. Serve.

CIOPPINO

½ c. chopped green pepper
½ c. chopped onion
2 medium cloves garlic, minced
¼ t. oregano, crushed
   Generous dash crushed leaf thyme
¼ c. olive oil
2 cans (10¾ oz. each) condensed tomato
   soup
1 c. water
½ c. Sauterne or other dry white wine
1 lb. shrimp, shelled and deveined
2 lobster tails, cooked (remove meat and
   cut in pieces)
2 T. chopped parsley
1 medium bay leaf
1 lb. haddock fillets, cut in 2-inch pieces

Cook green pepper, onion, garlic, oregano, and thyme in oil until tender. Add remaining ingredients except haddock. Cook over low heat for 10 minutes. Add haddock; cook 10 minutes more. Stir gently now and then. Serve from soup tureen.

BARBECUED SHORT RIBS

4 lbs. beef short ribs
2 t. salt
¼ t. pepper
1 8-oz. can tomato sauce
¼ c. catusp
⅓ c. brown sugar
¼ c. vinegar
2 T. prepared mustard
½ c. chopped onion
1 clove garlic, minced
1 T. chili powder

Place short ribs in covered frying pan on grill and cook slowly for 1½ hours, turning occasionally. Season with salt and pepper. Combine tomato sauce, catsup, brown sugar, vinegar, mustard, onion, garlic and chili powder in saucepan and simmer 5 minutes. Remove each short rib from pan, dip in sauce to coat all sides and place on grill, brushing with sauce and turning occasionally for 20 to 30 minutes or until done. 4 servings.

CHICKEN OLÉ

¼ c. butter
¼ c. oil
2 frying chickens, cut into serving pieces
   Water
2 onions (large), chopped
4 green peppers, chopped
1 qt. canned tomatoes with juice
2 cloves garlic, minced
   Salt
6 peppercorns
2 celery stalks with leaves
1 small carrot
¼ c. unbleached flour
2 c. ripe olives
2 c. canned corn
8 slices bacon

Brown chicken in butter and oil. Remove to kettle. Cover with water. Add the carrot, peppercorns, celery, garlic and salt. Heat to boiling and reduce to simmer. Cook until tender. Take meat from bones. Reserve 2 cups of chicken liquid. In the same pan in which the chicken was browned, cook the onions and green peppers until slightly soft. Add the liquid and flour and stir until thickened. Add tomatoes and olives. Layer the corn, chicken and tomato mixture in a casserole, top with bacon and place in a 375° oven for 25 to 30 minutes.

Patricia Mason

TEXAS PORK CHOPS

1 can condensed chili beef soup
1 c. cooked rice
2 T. finely chopped green pepper
2 T. sliced ripe olives
4 pork chops, ¾-inch thick
1 can (1 lb.) tomatoes
1 medium onion, sliced
1 medium clove garlic, minced

Combine ¼ cup soup, rice, green pepper and olives. Trim excess fat from chops. Slit each chop from outer edge toward bone, making a pocket; stuff with rice mixture. Fasten with toothpicks. In skillet, brown chops; pour off fat. Add remaining ingredients. Cover; cook over low heat 1¼ hours. Stir now and then to break up tomatoes. Uncover and cook to desired consistency.

SPANISH ENCHILADAS

½ c. cooking oil
3 T. flour
1 large can tomato juice
　Chili powder to taste
⅓ c. chopped onion
2 lbs. ground beef
1 c. Velveeta cheese
1 c. shredded cheddar cheese
1 small can diced olives
1 doz. flour tortillas

Brown meat and drain off liquid. Add chili powder to taste, onion, and chunks of Velveeta cheese. Set aside. Pour oil in a skillet and heat. When hot add flour a little at a time until thick and smooth. Add chili powder to taste. Remove from heat and add tomato juice. Watch carefully since sauce thickens fast. Stir constantly, adding tomato juice to make desired amount of sauce. Lightly grease a cookie sheet. Put tortillas on sheet, put a mixing spoon full of sauce on tortilla and place meat mixture on top of sauce. Roll up and place on far end of cookie sheet with split side down. Complete remaining tortillas. Pour sauce over all. Top with shredded cheddar cheese and diced olives. Bake at 300° until bubbly. Serve hot.

Suzanna C. Bascochea

TEXAS CHOCOLATE CAKE

Combine:

2 c. cake flour or 1¾ c. all-purpose flour
2 c. sugar
½ t. salt
1 t. baking soda
2 eggs
½ c. sour cream

Bring to a boil:

2 T. butter
1 c. water
4 T. cocoa

Add at once to the flour mixture; mix well and pour in greased oblong pan. Bake 20 minutes at 350°.

ICING

Combine 1 lb. powdered sugar, 1 t. vanilla and 1 c. chopped walnuts. Bring to a boil 1 T. butter, 6 T. milk and 4 T. cocoa. Add at once to powdered sugar mixture. Ice cake while hot.

Mrs. M. Biegel

SHRIMP CREOLE

½ c. chopped onion
½ c. chopped celery
1 clove garlic, minced
3 T. shortening
1 1-lb. can tomatoes
1 c. tomato sauce
1½ t. salt
1 t. sugar
2 T. curry
1 T. Worcestershire sauce
½ to 1 t. chili powder
　Dash of bottled hot pepper sauce
2 t. cornstarch
12 oz. frozen shelled shrimp, thawed
½ c. sliced fresh mushrooms or 1 can
½ c. chopped green pepper

In skillet cook onion, celery, mushroom and garlic in shortening till tender but not brown. Add tomatoes, tomato sauce and next 5 ingredients. Simmer uncovered for 45 minutes. Mix cornstarch with 1 tablespoon cold water. Stir into sauce. Cook and stir till mixture thickens and bubbles. Add shrimp and green pepper. Cover and simmer 5 minutes. Serve with parsley rice ring. Serves 6.

Margaret Gardner

CHICKEN CREOLE

2 chickens, 2 to 2½ lbs. each
¼ c. flour
1 t. salt
　Pepper
¼ t. paprika
¼ c. fat (chicken fat may be used)
½ c. chopped onion
½ c. water
¼ c. chopped green pepper
2½ c. fresh or canned tomatoes

Cut chickens into serving pieces. Roll in mixture of the flour, salt, pepper and paprika. Brown in melted fat. Add onion; cook 2 to 3 minutes. Add the water, cover and simmer about 30 minutes or until almost tender, adding more water if necessary. Stir occasionally to keep from sticking. Add green pepper and tomatoes. Simmer about 30 minutes longer. Serve on seasoned hot noodles or rice. Six servings.

Lemon Light Chiffon Cake

MISSOURI FROZEN CUSTARD

3 eggs
½ c. sugar
1 qt. milk, scalded
½ t. vanilla
⅛ t. salt
⅛ t. nutmeg
   Toasted coconut and cherries

Beat eggs and sugar until thickened. Add scalded milk slowly to eggs. Cook, stirring, in top of double boiler until mixture coats spoon.

Add vanilla, salt and nutmeg. Cool. If custard separates when it stands, smooth with further beating. Partially freeze, stirring several times while in freezer section. Ice particles should be evenly distributed throughout the custard. Spoon into dessert bowls and top with whipped cream, toasted coconut, and a cherry. Serves 8.

Estella Long Black

TEXAS PECAN CAKE

Cream:

  2 c. sugar
  1 lb. butter or margarine
  6 eggs (add one at a time)

Sift and add:

3½ c. flour
1½ t. baking powder
  1 t. salt

Add:

  2 T. lemon extract

Mix fruits and nuts with:

½ c. flour
1 lb. white raisins
1 lb. pecans (chopped or whole)
6 oz. candied cherries (chopped or whole)
6 oz. candied pineapple (chopped)

Add to cake batter.

Bake in 10-inch tube pan in a 300° oven for 2½ to 3 hours. Note: You may use waxed paper or foil on top of pan to keep cake from drying out. Remove before cake is fully baked so top can brown. Cool cake in pan.

Mrs. Glenn Butler

LEMON LIGHT CHIFFON CAKE

2¼ c. cake flour
  1 c. sugar
  1 T. baking powder
  1 t. salt
½ c. salad oil
  5 egg yolks
¾ c. cold water
  2 t. grated lemon rind
  2 t. vanilla extract
  1 c. egg whites (about 7 egg whites)
½ t. cream of tartar
½ c. sugar
  Lemon Filling

Combine flour, 1 cup sugar, baking powder and salt in large mixing bowl. Make a well in center of dry ingredients. Add oil, egg yolks, water, lemon rind and vanilla. Beat until smooth. Beat egg whites with cream of tartar until soft peaks form. Gradually add ½ cup sugar, beating constantly until egg whites stand in stiff, glossy peaks. Pour egg yolk mixture over egg whites, a little at a time, folding in after each addition. Mix only until blended. Turn into ungreased 10-inch tube pan. Bake in a 325° oven for 60 to 70 minutes, or until cake springs back when lightly touched. Invert pan and cool cake thoroughly before removing. Cut into three equal layers. Spread top of each layer with ⅓ of Lemon Filling.

LEMON FILLING

1 c. sugar
3 T. cornstarch
  Dash of salt
1 c. cold water
2 egg yolks, slightly beaten
2 t. grated lemon rind
¼ c. lemon juice
1 T. butter

Combine sugar, cornstarch and salt in saucepan; gradually stir in water. Blend in egg yolks, lemon rind and juice. Cook over medium heat, stirring constantly until mixture boils. Boil one minute, stirring constantly. Remove from heat and blend in butter. Cool to room temperature without stirring.

WEST

WASHINGTON

OREGON   UTAH

IDAHO   ARIZONA

MONTANA   NEW MEXICO

WYOMING   NEVADA

COLORADO   CALIFORNIA

FRONTIER BEAN DIP

1 #2 can pork and beans in tomato sauce
¼ c. shredded American cheese
½ t. garlic salt
½ t. chili powder
  Pinch salt
  Dash of pepper
1 t. wine vinegar
5 slices bacon, fried crisp and crumbled

Combine all ingredients except bacon. Heat thoroughly. Sprinkle with the crumbled bacon and serve with corn chips.

GUACAMOLE DIP

1 large ripe avocado
1 medium tomato
2 t. grated onion
1 t. lemon juice
  Salt and pepper to taste
1 clove garlic, minced
1 c. dairy sour cream

Peel avocado and remove pit. Place avocado meat in bowl, mash with fork and add the peeled and minced tomato, onion, lemon juice, salt, pepper and garlic. Blend in the sour cream.

MOUNTAINS

Dan Hoover

There's a majesty to mountains
Rolled and tumbled, reaching high
Up through wispy white-cloud vapors
To a deep blue bowl of sky.

Bright green trees spread to adorn them,
Sparkling streams of water fall
Bubbling, ice-cold, foaming, splashing...
Adding beauty to it all.

Oh, how bracing is the pine scent
And the cold clean atmosphere,
Mixed with melody of bird notes
Ringing sweet and crystal clear.

On those little mountain meadows
Fenced by quaking aspen trees,
Deer and fawn graze in the bounty
Of green grass up to their knees.

Layered, rainbow-tinted sandstones
Testify to ages past,
Beautiful and reassuring
That our earth will always last.

POTATO AND SPINACH SOUP

¼ c. chopped onion
2 T. butter or margarine
2 c. water
1 t. salt
2 c. finely cut potatoes
2 c. chopped, fresh or frozen spinach
1 13-oz. can evaporated milk
1 t. Worcestershire sauce
Shredded cheese

Sauté onion in butter until tender. Add water, salt, potatoes and spinach. Cook until potatoes are tender, about 20 minutes. Add milk and Worcestershire sauce. Heat well but do not boil. Serve with shredded cheese in each bowl.

CALIFORNIA SALAD BOWL

2 c. head lettuce
1 c. romaine
½ c. celery, sliced thin
¼ c. green onions, sliced
1 can (5 oz.) lobster, drained
¾ c. cherry tomatoes, halved
1 grapefruit, sectioned
1 avocado, sliced
5 pitted ripe olives, sliced
¼ c. fresh lemon juice

In a large salad bowl toss together lettuce, romaine, celery and onions. Arrange lobster, tomatoes, grapefruit sections, avocado and olive slices on top of greens. Sprinkle with lemon juice. Cover and chill. Serve with the following dressing.

CREAM DRESSING

1½ c. cottage cheese
⅓ c. dairy sour cream
1 t. grated lemon rind
Salt and pepper

In a small mixing bowl beat cottage cheese until fairly smooth, using high speed of mixer. Add sour cream and lemon rind. Salt and pepper to taste.

CALIFORNIA CRAB SALAD

1 c. chili sauce
2 T. lemon juice
1 T. prepared horseradish
⅛ t. garlic powder
2 T. chopped green onion
⅛ t. dried dill
½ c. wine
1 lb. fresh crabmeat
Lettuce or other greens
Ripe olives and hard-cooked eggs

Mix together the chili sauce, lemon juice, horseradish, garlic powder, onion, dill and wine. Refrigerate for several hours. Add half of the crabmeat to sauce, and place on lettuce on individual plates. Top with remaining crabmeat. Garnish with hard-cooked eggs and olives. The extra sauce may be served separately, if desired.

SALMON CASSEROLE

2 12-oz. pkgs. frozen salmon steaks, thawed (other fresh or frozen fish steaks may be substituted)
3 c. bread cubes
⅓ c. chopped green pepper
2 T. chopped parsley
1 T. chopped onion
Pinch thyme
¼ c. butter
3 T. flour
½ t. salt
⅛ t. pepper
⅛ t. dry mustard
1½ c. milk
¼ t. Worcestershire sauce
1 t. lemon juice
Paprika

Mix together the bread cubes, green pepper, parsley, onion and thyme and cover bottom of shallow, buttered casserole.

Melt butter in saucepan and stir in flour, salt, pepper and mustard. Remove from heat and gradually stir in the milk. Cook until thickened, stirring constantly, then cook 2 more minutes. Add Worcestershire sauce.

Place fish steaks on the bread mixture, sprinkle with lemon juice and pour sauce over all. Sprinkle with a little paprika. Bake at 375° for about 25 minutes.

Photo courtesy General Foods Corporation

CARE-LESS BRISKET OF BEEF

Here's a recipe for those Sundays when you couldn't care less about cooking, but you've got either house guests or a hungry family.

1¾ c. (18-oz. bottle) Open Pit Barbecue Sauce
5 lb. (about) brisket of beef

Pour barbecue sauce over meat in a shallow roasting pan. Cover and bake at 325° for 4 hours or until tender, basting occasionally to glaze meat. Pour or skim fat from drippings. Serve drippings as sauce for meat. Makes 8 to 10 servings.

Note: Recipe may be doubled, using 2 briskets of beef (about 5 pounds each).

And all the trimmings: Brussels sprouts, sliced tomatoes and red onion rings, French bread and whatever dessert comes to mind or hand. Chocolate cake, maybe?

POACHED SALMON

**1 4-lb. piece of fresh salmon,
skinned and boned**

In a large pan or a fish pan place about 2 quarts of water, or enough to cover the fish.

Add:

**1 t. salt
Dash of pepper
1 lemon, sliced
4 stalks of celery, chopped
1 medium onion, sliced**

Bring to a boil, then add salmon and simmer gently for about 20 minutes or until fish flakes when tested with a fork. Cool in the stock, remove and drain on toweling. Place in refrigerator and chill. Hint: You might want to wrap the fish in a piece of cheesecloth so that it can be easily removed from the stock. Do not overcook. The fish may be covered with mayonnaise to which curry powder has been added, then garnished with ripe olives, sliced cucumbers and pimiento.

BAKED WHOLE SALMON

1 large salmon, about 10 to 15 pounds

Rub fish with salt, pepper and lemon, then wrap in brown wrapping paper or foil. Bake slowly at 250 to 275° for three hours or until done. Remove paper and skin. Place on large platter and serve with melted butter and lemon.

SALMON LOAF

**2 c. flaked cooked salmon
½ c. fine bread crumbs
4 T. butter
2 eggs, slightly beaten
1 T. minced parsley
Salt and pepper to taste**

Combine ingredients. Steam 1 hour in buttered mold or bake in pan of hot water in 375° oven. Serve hot or cold. Serves 6.

Laurie Williams

LITTLE SALMON PIES

Drain 1 large can of salmon, red or pink, reserving liquid. Remove the bones and skin. Place the reserved fish liquid in a measuring cup and add milk to make 1 cup. In a saucepan heat 4 T. butter and when hot but not browned remove from heat. Immediately add 4 T. of flour. Blend until smooth. Then return to the heat and simmer a few minutes.

Add the 1 c. of salmon liquid and milk plus one more cup of milk. Cook until it begins to thicken, then add the salmon which has been broken up into bite-size pieces. No salt is needed, but you can season it according to your preference with pepper, spices or herbs. I use pepper and ¼ t. powdered cloves or rosemary.

When the mixture is heated through, fill 3 individual casseroles, each holding about a cupful and cover with your favorite pie crust or biscuit dough.

Bake at 400° for 15 to 20 minutes or as long as it takes to brown the crust.

The trick to getting smooth white sauce is to have the butter hot when you add the flour and always add it when the pan is *off* the heat.

Sister M. Blanche Aubuchon

FISH STEW

**1 lb. fish fillets, fresh or frozen
1 c. chopped onion
⅓ c. melted fat
1 can tomatoes (1 lb., 12 oz.)
2 c. potatoes, cut into small pieces
1 c. water
¼ c. catsup
½ t. salt
Pepper to season
1 can mixed vegetables (1 lb.)**

If the fish fillets are frozen, let them thaw. Skin the fillets. Cut them into pieces about an inch square. In a large skillet fry the onion in the fat until cooked. Add the tomatoes, potatoes, water, catsup, salt and pepper. Cover and simmer for 30 minutes. Add the fish, mixed vegetables and vegetable liquid. Cover and simmer about 15 minutes longer or until the potatoes are fully cooked.

WESTERN BAKED BEANS

3 c. dried kidney beans
1 clove garlic, minced
4 slices bacon, cut in pieces
2 small onions
½ c. brown sugar
1 T. salt
1 T. chili powder
1 can tomato soup

Wash beans and soak them overnight. Drain and rinse. Place in large kettle and cover with water. Add garlic. Cook slowly for one hour. Drain and reserve liquid. Place beans in bean pot. Add bacon and onions. Then mix together brown sugar, salt and chili powder and sprinkle over beans. Combine tomato soup with one soup can of reserved bean liquid. Pour over beans. Cover bean pot and bake at 300° for 5 hours. Add more of reserved liquid if necessary. Serves 8 to 10.

Mrs. Hugh L. Pickett

FRIED BEANS
(FRIJOLES FRITOS)

1 lb. pinto beans
4 T. butter

Soak beans overnight, drain and cover with fresh, salted water. Boil until beans are done. Drain and mash the beans. Melt butter in a skillet and fry beans. Serve with tacos.

Doc Kingsley

MONTERREY BAKE

1 lb. lean ground beef
1 t. each garlic and onion powders
1½ t. salt
¼ t. hot liquid pepper
1 T. lemon juice
½ c. mayonnaise
3 c. cooked rice
1 c. sliced celery
½ c. chopped green pepper
2 medium tomatoes, cut in eighths
1 c. crushed corn chips

Sauté meat with garlic and onion powders in a lightly greased skillet about 10 minutes, or until done. Blend salt, liquid pepper, lemon juice and mayonnaise. Add this mixture and remaining ingredients to ground beef. Turn into a greased 2-quart casserole. Top with corn chips. Bake at 375° for 25 to 30 minutes. Makes 6 servings.

CHICKEN SPECIAL

1 whole chicken
1 doz. corn tortillas
1 can cream of mushroom soup
1 can cream of chicken soup
1 c. milk
1 onion, grated
1 can green chili sauce
½ c. cheddar cheese, grated

Roast the chicken in foil at 400° for one hour. Cool. Remove meat from bones and cut into bite-size pieces. Blend with soups, milk, onion and chili sauce. Cut tortillas into large pieces and line a 13 x 9-inch pan. Alternate layers of sauce with tortillas. Top with cheese. Place in refrigerator overnight. Bake 1 hour at 325°.

Mrs. Mary Biegel

HASH RANCHERO

6 oz. lean ground beef
⅓ c. each chopped onion and green pepper
1 t. chili powder
1 t. salt
¼ t. each pepper and garlic powder
1 10-oz. can tomatoes, well drained
1 c. cooked rice

In a small oven-proof skillet sauté beef, onion, green pepper and seasonings until meat is no longer pink and vegetables are tender. Stir frequently to crumble meat. Add tomatoes and rice. Bake at 350° for 20 minutes or until thoroughly heated. Makes 2 servings.

BEEF AND BEANS

2 1-lb. cans pork and beans
1 T. prepared mustard
½ c. catsup
½ c. brown sugar
1 T. Worcestershire sauce
1 medium onion, chopped
½ lb. ground beef

Mix beans with mustard, catsup, sugar, Worcestershire sauce and onion. Brown meat. Add to bean mixture. Bake 45 minutes at 400°.

Mrs. Merlyn Rensberry

CHILI

2 c. cooked pinto beans
½ lb. pork sausage
1½ lbs. ground beef
1 qt. tomato juice
1 clove garlic
3 whole cloves
1 t. paprika
4 T. chili powder
1 bay leaf
   Salt and cayenne pepper to taste
1 large onion, chopped

Cook crumbled sausage over medium heat till done but not brown. Add onion and ground beef and cook slowly till it changes color. Place in large kettle and add remaining ingredients. Simmer for 1 hour. Remove cloves and garlic before serving.

Mrs. Blair Cunningham

FROSTED CORNED BEEF LOAF

1 12-oz. can corned beef, chilled
2 8-oz. pkgs. cream cheese
1 c. mayonnaise
1 T. Worcestershire sauce
½ t. tabasco sauce

Cut chilled corned beef horizontally into 3 or 4 layers. Blend cream cheese with remaining ingredients until smooth. Spread mixture generously between corned beef slices. Form into loaf and cover with remaining cheese spread. Refrigerate. To serve, slice chilled loaf with a sharp knife.

BAKED CHEESE TOMATOES

4 to 6 large, firm tomatoes
½ lb. cheddar cheese, cubed
1 c. toasted bread cubes
½ t. nutmeg
¼ t. salt
1 T. parsley flakes
½ c. chopped cashew nuts
2 T. butter, melted
¼ c. finely chopped onion
1 c. diced tomato pulp

Core and scoop out tomatoes. Sprinkle lightly with salt. Combine cheddar cheese, bread cubes, nutmeg, salt, parsley flakes, nuts, butter, onion and tomato pulp. Fill tomatoes with cheese mixture and wrap each in aluminum foil. Bake 15 minutes at 350°.

PEPPER-PARSLEY GREEN RICE

¾ c. butter
2 c. cooked rice
2 c. sharp cheese, shredded
2 eggs, beaten
2 c. milk
1 c. chopped parsley or ½ c. dried parsley
1 green pepper, chopped
1 clove garlic, chopped, or use flakes
   Chopped onion, salt and pepper to taste

Add butter to hot rice, then the cheese, beaten eggs and milk. Add rest of ingredients and place in buttered casserole. Bake at 350° for 30 minutes.

Ione Jordan

STEWED OKRA AND TOMATOES

1 small onion, chopped
2 T. oil
1 10-oz. pkg. frozen okra
1 16-oz. can tomatoes
½ t. salt
¼ t. pepper

Cook onion in fat in saucepan over moderate heat until lightly browned.

Add remaining ingredients and cook until okra is tender and mixture thickens, 10 to 15 minutes. Stir occasionally to prevent sticking.

PEACH PUDDING

Peaches, sliced	**1 c. flour**
¾ **c. sugar**	**Pinch of salt**
1 egg	**1 t. baking powder**
2 T. shortening	**1 t. vanilla**
½ **c. milk**	

Butter a glass pie plate. Fill plate with sliced peaches. Combine remaining ingredients and pour over peaches. Bake at 350° for 30 minutes or until cake tester inserted in center of pudding comes out clean.

Judith E. Bray

YAKIMA APPLE PUDDING

½ c. margarine	1 c. flour
½ c. sugar	1 t. baking soda
½ c. light corn	1 t. nutmeg
syrup	¼ t. salt
1 egg	2 c. chopped apples
1 c. nutmeats	

Blend margarine, sugar and syrup. Add egg and beat well. Sift dry ingredients and stir into creamed mixture. Mix apples and nuts and stir into batter. Pour into a greased 9-inch square baking pan. Bake at 350° for about 45 minutes or until done. Serve warm or cold with the following sauce.

BUTTER SAUCE

Cream ½ cup butter or margarine. Gradually cream in 1 cup sifted confectioners' sugar until light and fluffy. Slowly stir 1 cup cold water into 1 tablespoon cornstarch. Cook and stir until thick and clear. Stir hot mixture into creamed mixture. Add 1 teaspoon vinegar and 1½ teaspoons vanilla. Serve warm.

Bonnie Lobdell

PEACH PIE

1 unbaked pie shell
  Peaches
1 c. half-and-half or light cream
1 c. sugar
3 T. flour
¾ t. cornstarch

Peel and slice peaches. Place in pie shell. Combine remaining ingredients and pour over peaches. Place lattice top over pie and bake at 350° for 40 to 50 minutes.

Juanita Patrick

FRESH GOOSEBERRY PIE

Prepare pastry for a two-crust 9-inch pie and line pie plate with pastry.

½ c. crushed gooseberries
1½ c. sugar
3 T. quick-cooking tapioca
¼ t. salt

Combine ingredients. Cook and stir till mixture thickens and boils. Add 2½ cups whole gooseberries. Pour into pastry shell. Dot with 2 tablespoons butter or margarine. Adjust top crust, cutting slits for steam to escape. Seal. Bake in a 400° oven for 30 to 40 minutes or till crust is nicely browned. Serve warm.

Verna Sparks

APPLE CRISP

PART 1

2 T. granulated sugar
¼ t. cinnamon
4 c. tart apples, pared and sliced
¼ c. water

Mix sugar with cinnamon. Add apples, arrange in a buttered 8-inch square pan and sprinkle with the water.

PART 2

3 T. softened butter or margarine
½ c. flour
⅛ t. salt
¼ t. cinnamon
¼ t. nutmeg
⅓ c. brown sugar, packed

Mix butter with flour, sugar, cinnamon, nutmeg and salt. Spread over apples. Bake uncovered at 350° for 40 minutes or until lightly browned and apples are tender.

Serve with whipped cream.

NECTARINE NUT LOAF

2 or 3 fresh nectarines
½ c. margarine
1 c. sugar
2 eggs
1 t. vanilla
2½ c. sifted flour
2½ t. baking powder
1 t. salt
½ c. chopped pecans or diced roasted almonds

Peel nectarines. Mash enough fruit to measure 1 cup. Cream margarine with sugar. Add eggs and vanilla. Sift flour with baking powder and salt. Add to creamed mixture alternately with mashed nectarines, mixing well after each addition. Blend in nuts. Turn into greased and floured loaf pan; bake in 350° oven about 1 hour. Cool in pan 10 minutes; remove and finish cooling on rack. This loaf is best when served the next day.

ORANGE TORTE

1 c. sugar
1 c. butter
1 c. golden raisins
¼ lb. pecans, coarsely chopped
2 eggs
Grated rind of 2 oranges
1 t. vanilla
Pinch of salt
1 c. sour cream or sour half-and-half
1 t. baking soda
1 t. baking powder
2½ c. cake flour

Cream butter and sugar, add eggs and mix well. Add other ingredients alternately. Bake in a spring pan 1 hour and 35 minutes in a 325° oven.

Stir juice of 1 orange with ½ cup sugar until dissolved. About 10 minutes after removing from oven, pour 4 to 5 teaspoons of juice over it until absorbed.

Mrs. Walter A. Platzke

APPLE BUTTER SPICE CAKE

2 c. flour	2 eggs
1 t. baking powder	¾ c. apple butter
1 t. baking soda	1 t. vanilla
½ t. salt	½ c. whole bran
½ c. margarine	cereal
1 c. sugar	1 c. sour cream

TOPPING MIX

½ c. brown sugar	1 t. cinnamon
½ t. nutmeg	½ c. nutmeats

Mix together.

Blend margarine, sugar and eggs and beat well. Stir in apple butter, vanilla and cereal. Add sifted dry ingredients alternately with sour cream. Begin and end with dry ingredients. Spread half of the batter in greased 9 x 13-inch pan; sprinkle half of Topping Mix over batter. Add remaining batter and sprinkle with remaining Topping Mix.

This is a moist cake and keeps well for several days. It does not require a frosting.

Mrs. N. W. Sackett

FIG BREAD

2½ c. flour
4 t. baking powder
½ t. salt
½ c. sugar
1¼ c. figs (cut in small pieces)
1¼ c. milk
2 eggs
2 T. melted shortening

Sift flour with baking powder, salt and sugar. Add figs. Combine well-beaten eggs with milk and add to dry ingredients. Add melted shortening. Pour into greased 1 pound loaf pan. Allow to stand 20 minutes before baking. Bake 1 hour in moderate (350°) oven. Yield: 1 pound loaf.

Mary T. Dougan

POTATO CANDY

½ c. cold mashed potatoes
4 c. sifted confectioners' sugar (or enough to make fondant easy to handle)
Pinch of salt
½ t. vanilla

Mix well, then turn out on a piece of waxed paper and roll into a rectangle about ¼-inch thick. Spread with ½ c. peanut butter, creamy or chunk style. Roll up like a jelly roll and chill for about 8 hours. Cut into ¼-inch thick slices.

Mary A. Miller

PEAR CHIPS JAM

7 c. sugar
4 c. water
2 oz. candied ginger
2 lemons, sliced thin
4 lbs. pears, peeled and sliced thin

Make a syrup of the sugar and water. Add finely chopped ginger, lemons and pears. Simmer, stirring frequently, for about 1¾ hours. Pour into jelly glasses or jars. Seal or cover with paraffin.

Mrs. Rosalie L. Kennedy

HICKORY NUT CAKE

1½ c. sugar
½ c. butter or margarine
½ c. milk
2 c. sifted flour
2 t. baking powder
½ t. nutmeg
¼ t. salt
1 c. hickory nuts, chopped fine
3 egg whites, stiffly beaten

Mix sugar and shortening. Combine sifted flour with other dry ingredients. Add to shortening mixture alternately with milk. Add nut meats and stir well. Fold in beaten egg whites. Bake in a 350° oven in 2 layers or 1 square loaf pan.

WHITE SAUCE FROSTING

½ c. butter
½ c. flour
¼ t. salt
½ c. milk
2½ c. powdered sugar
½ t. vanilla

Melt butter slowly in saucepan. Remove from heat. Blend in flour and salt. Stir in the milk. Bring to a boil, stirring constantly about 1 minute. Cool to lukewarm. Stir in powdered sugar and vanilla. Beat until of spreading consistency. Sprinkle coconut or chopped nuts on top of frosting. This is enough for a 2-layer cake.

T. Colwill

POTATO CAKE

⅔ c. margarine
2 c. sugar
4 eggs, separated
3 oz. unsweetened chocolate, melted, or 3 heaping t. cocoa
1 c. mashed potatoes
2½ c. flour
2½ t. baking powder
½ c. milk
1 c. raisins
1 c. finely chopped nuts

Cream margarine, add sugar gradually and cream well. Beat in egg yolks one at a time. Add chocolate and potatoes. Sift dry ingredients together and add to creamed mixture alternately with milk. Stir in raisins and nuts. Fold in stiffly beaten egg whites. Turn batter into a greased tube pan and bake at 400° for 50 minutes or until cake tests done.

Effie Willis

SAGEBRUSH AND SAND

Only sagebrush and sand they say,
No beauty can they see,
Yet the distant snowcapped mountains
Are beautiful to me.

A meadowlark in the bushes
So sweetly sings at dawn
That I am thrilled with such rapture,
My own heart echoes the song.

The rugged beauty of morning,
Hills bathed in pure sunlight,
Is only surpassed at evening
By shadows that deepen to night.

The moonlight silvers the sagebrush
And gemlike the sand is aglow,
And the stars in sparkling glory
Shine down on the scene below.

Cora V. Feese

Hawaiian Ham Slices

58

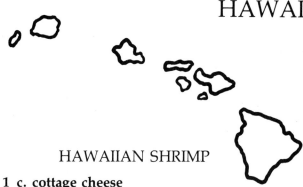

HAWAIIAN HAM SLICES

2 center ham steaks, 1 inch thick
1 c. drained crushed pineapple
1 c. mixed chopped fruit (light raisins, maraschino cherries, cooked prunes)
1 c. brown sugar
1 c. pineapple chunks
¼ c. pecan halves
½ c. maraschino cherries
Mandarin orange sections

Place a sheet of heavy-duty foil in a shallow aluminum pan and place one ham steak in center. Gash fat at 1-inch intervals so ham will stay flat. Combine crushed pineapple with chopped fruit and half the brown sugar. Spread half this mixture over the steak. Top with the second steak, sandwich fashion. Fold foil loosely around ham slices. Bake in 400° F. oven for 45 minutes. Remove from oven and roll back foil. Spoon out fat. Top with remaining fruit mixture, the pineapple chunks, pecans, cherries, orange sections and remaining brown sugar. Return to oven for 20 minutes to glaze, basting occasionally with liquid.

HAWAIIAN HAM RING

Sauce

3 T. brown sugar
2 T. vinegar
½ c. pineapple syrup
¼ t. mustard

Mix and bring to a boil.

Ham Rings

1 lb. ground ham
1 lb. ground pork
2 eggs
1 c. cornflake crumbs
1 c. milk
1 can sliced pineapple

Combine all ingredients except pineapple. Shape in form of doughnuts; place each on drained pineapple ring. Bake at 325° for 1 hour and 15 minutes, basting frequently with sauce.

If desired, grated cheese may be sprinkled on top just before they are removed from the oven.

Mrs. R. C. Sauer

HAWAIIAN SHRIMP

1 c. cottage cheese
1 7-oz. pkg. frozen shrimp, cooked, cleaned and cut in small pieces
¼ c. chopped celery
1 c. crushed pineapple, well drained
2 t. lemon juice
½ t. salt

Beat cottage cheese at highest speed of mixer until smooth. Add shrimp, celery, pineapple, lemon juice and salt. Chill. This can be used as a sandwich filling, or for an open face sandwich. Garnish with sliced, stuffed olives.

HAWAII

At the close of day this island paradise
. . . Full of quiet beauty,
Closes the eyes of the sky
With many-colored clouds.
Hawaii, land of dreams,
Inspiration for poetic verses,
Land of fragrant flowers . . .
Romantic legends,
My heart goes out to you, beautiful island,
Upon whose shores white sand blazes
  in the sun . . .
A peaceful beauty when day is done!
Giant palms wave in the breeze,
Seeming to touch the sky.
. . . I yearn to touch such beauty.
Oh, that I could be the breeze . . .
Gently caressing the palm trees,
Rearranging clouds in intricate patterns,
Blowing upon the sandy beaches
Or the wind behind each wave.

Sara Mae Higgs

HAWAIIAN SALAD

8 cooked lobster tails
¼ c. butter
¼ c. lemon juice
¼ c. light brown sugar
½ c. commercial sour cream
1 c. green grapes, seeded and cut in half
1 c. cottage cheese
½ c. chopped celery
½ t. salt
1 fresh pineapple
  Lettuce

Remove meat from lobster tails and break into bite-sized pieces. Cover and chill. Melt butter and add lemon juice and brown sugar. Heat to boiling. Remove from stove, add lobster pieces and chill. Peel pineapple and cut into spears. Fold sour cream into lobster mixture. Blend in grapes, cottage cheese, celery and salt.

Crack backs of lobster tails and place 2 tails together on lettuce. Mound about 1¼ cups of mixture into tails. Serve with pineapple spears and garnish with additional grapes.

LEMON DREAM ICE CREAM

One cup of sugar, then juice and rind
Of one lemon if you'd be so kind.

Then add one pint of coffee cream
And there you have my lemon dream!

Pop it in your freezing tray,
That's all you do, now you can play!

You never stir, just "leave it be!"
It's always smooth in hours three!

Mary Colby Wilder

COCONUT POUND CAKE

½ lb. butter or margarine
½ c. vegetable shortening
3 c. sugar
3 c. all-purpose flour
6 eggs
1 t. coconut flavoring
½ t. brandy flavoring
1 c. milk
1 can flaked coconut

Cream butter, shortening and sugar until light and fluffy. Add eggs one at a time, beating after each one. Add flavoring and mix well. Add flour and milk alternately. Stir in coconut. Bake at 350° for 1¼ hours.

Use either a 16-inch loaf pan or two 9-inch pans.

Zyra B. Walker

HAWAIIAN LEMON PIE

¼ c. firmly packed brown sugar
3 T. melted butter or margarine
¾ c. crushed pineapple, well drained
¼ c. flaked coconut
1 pkg. lemon pie filling mix
¾ c. granulated sugar
2 c. cold water
2 eggs, separated
2 T. lemon juice
1 9-inch unbaked pie shell
  (pricked with fork tines on bottom
  and around the sides)

Combine brown sugar with 2 T. of melted butter. Add crushed pineapple and coconut, mix well and spread in pie shell. Bake at 425° for about 15 minutes or until lightly browned. Remove from oven and cool. Combine pie filling mix with ½ c. sugar, add 2 c. water and yolks of 2 eggs, well beaten. Cook in double boiler, stirring constantly, until thickened. Remove from stove, add remaining tablespoon melted butter and 2 T. lemon juice. Cool well, stirring occasionally.

Beat egg whites with remaining ¼ c. sugar, until they stand in soft peaks. Fold into cooled pudding and pour over mixture in pie shell. Chill thoroughly before serving.

BROILED VENISON STEAK

Venison steaks are treated very much like beef. Steaks ¾ inch or 1 inch thick are best for broiling. Broil to your preference, and season with salt, pepper and butter. For added flavor serve with currant or wild plum jelly.

Venison steak may also be prepared as a Swiss steak. When browned, add tomatoes to cover, chopped onions, pinch of thyme and salt and pepper to taste. Simmer until tender. Tomatoes help to overcome the wild taste of venison.

VENISON SALAD

    4 c. cooked venison, cut in small cubes
       French dressing
    1 c. celery, sliced
    ½ c. stuffed olives, sliced, or ripe olives
    4 hard-cooked eggs, sliced
       Mayonnaise
       Lettuce

Marinate the cubed venison in the French dressing for 1 hour in the refrigerator, stirring occasionally. Drain excess French dressing and combine with all other ingredients, except mayonnaise, lettuce and a few olives and egg slices. Season to taste. Place lettuce in salad bowl. Add venison salad, top with mayonnaise and garnish with reserved egg slices and stuffed olives.

CRANBERRY CATSUP

2½ lbs. cranberries   2 T. cinnamon
  5 c. vinegar   1 t. cloves
2½ c. sugar

Cook cranberries in vinegar until they burst open. Rub through a sieve, add sugar and spices, simmer until thick and seal in sterilized jars. Makes 3 pints.

SALMONBURGERS

    1 1-lb. can salmon
    ½ c. chopped onion
    ¼ c. melted butter or margarine
    ⅓ c. dry bread crumbs
    2 eggs, beaten
    1 t. prepared mustard
    ½ t. salt
    ½ c. dry bread crumbs
    6 hamburger rolls

Drain the liquid from the salmon and reserve. Break salmon into small pieces. Sauté the onion in the butter. Mix onion, ⅓ cup bread crumbs, eggs, mustard, salt, salmon, and salmon liquid. Form into cakes and roll in the ½ cup bread crumbs. Fry in hot fat for 3 to 4 minutes or until brown. Turn carefully. Fry 3 to 4 minutes longer or until brown. Drain on paper toweling. Place on bottom half of a hamburger roll and cover with the top half of roll.

VENISON MEAT LOAF

    2 lbs. ground lean venison
    ¼ lb. salt pork, cut in small pieces
    3 stalks celery, chopped
    2 T. chopped parsley
    1 small onion, chopped
    4 T. flour
    1 c. milk
    2 eggs, slightly beaten
    1 c. soft bread crumbs
    1 t. salt
       Dash of pepper

Fry salt pork until crisp. Add celery, parsley and onion and cook slightly. Stir in flour. Gradually add milk and cook until thickened. Combine all ingredients and pack into a greased loaf pan. Bake at 375° for about 1½ hours.

Fireside Bliss *Vegetable Jumble Salad* *Garlic Herbed Bread Chunks*

FIRESIDE SUPPER

After a day in the open it's fun to come home to a warm and hearty supper served in front of the fire. You'll be so comfortable and cozy, with just a few last minute touches to add to the food.

Much of the delicious food pictured can be prepared the night before. The main dish can go into the oven before you leave. As soon as you get home, zip the bread chunks into the oven and put finishing touches on the salad. Carry it all to the low fireside table and enjoy this delicious fireside supper.

FIRESIDE BLISS

2 lbs. boneless beef chuck, cut 1 inch thick
1 envelope beef flavor mushroom
   soup mix
1 1-lb. can tomatoes, drained and chopped
¼ t. salt
   Generous sprinkling pepper
1 T. cornstarch
½ c. juice from tomatoes
6 small onions, peeled
4 carrots—scraped and quartered

Tear off a 20-inch sheet of heavy-duty aluminum foil and place on a shallow pan. With a sharp knife, cut beef into serving portions. Arrange the slices on the foil, slightly overlapping them. Sprinkle with the soup mix and spoon the tomatoes over the meat. Mix seasonings and cornstarch with tomato juice and pour over meat and tomatoes. Arrange the onions and carrots around the meat. Bring two long ends of the foil up over the meat and seal with a double fold. Seal remaining ends in the same way to make a tight package. Refrigerate if prepared the night before serving. When ready to bake, place on a middle shelf in the oven. Bake 2 hours at 350° or 5 hours at 250°. To serve, transfer package to a shallow basket or tray. Open the package and turn back the foil, crimping edges to make an attractive border.

GARLIC HERBED BREAD CHUNKS

1 large loaf Italian bread
¼ lb. butter or margarine
¼ t. oregano
¼ t. paprika
1 clove garlic
1 t. parsley flakes or
   1 T. chopped fresh parsley
4 T. grated Parmesan cheese

Cut bread in half lengthwise through the center. Cut bread in thick 2-inch slices, then cut each slice into quarters to make chunks. Have the butter or margarine at room temperature so it is soft. Use a garlic press to crush the garlic, letting the juice run into the butter. Add all the other seasonings and mix together. Spread butter on all sides of bread chunks. Place on a large sheet of foil and gather foil up around the bread to make a package. Refrigerate until shortly before serving. Partially open the foil and heat the bread in the oven with the meat for 30 minutes. Turn back the foil and crimp edges to make a pretty container for the hot, savory chunks.

VEGETABLE JUMBLE SALAD

2 10-oz. pkgs. frozen mixed vegetables
1 pt. cherry tomatoes
1 head Boston lettuce
1 7-oz. pkg. creamy blue cheese salad
   dressing mix

Cook frozen vegetables according to package directions. Place them in a plastic or ceramic bowl, cover with foil and refrigerate until cold. Rinse and refrigerate cherry tomatoes, leaving stems on if they are fresh and green. Wash lettuce, shake off water, place on paper towels to absorb last drops of moisture and wrap in foil. Prepare blue cheese dressing according to package directions and pour over chilled mixed vegetables, tossing very lightly with a fork. Return to refrigerator. Just before serving, arrange lettuce leaves around the outside of a salad bowl, heap the mixed vegetables in center and border with the cherry tomatoes.

INDEX

APPETIZERS
Chili Dip, 39
Frontier Bean Dip, 48
Guacamole Dip, 48

BREADS
Chippewa Indian Fried Bread, 29
Corn Bread, 18
Fastnachts, 10
Fig Bread, 56
Garlic Herbed Bread Chunks, 63
Hush Puppies, 18
Molasses Pumpkin Bread, 10
Nectarine Nut Loaf, 55
Never-Fail Nutbread, 10
Quick Praline Rolls, 14
Root Beer Bread, 16
South Carolina Spoon Bread, 18

CAKES
Apple Butter Spice Cake, 56
Apple Cake, 34
Apple Chip Cake, 9
Blueberry Cheese Slices, 35
Coconut Pound Cake, 60
Crumb Cake, 35
Dainty Tea Cakes, 22
Franklin Nut Cake, 22
Hickory Nut Cake, 57
Lemon Light Chiffon Cake, 47
Mama's Molasses Cakes, 9
New England Molasses Cake, 8
Orange Blossoms, 21
Orange Date Cake, 21
Orange Torte, 56
Pecan Fruit Cake, 22
Potato Cake, 57
Salted Peanut Cake, 24
Strawberry Shortcake, 31
Sweet Potato Cake, 24
Texas Chocolate Cake, 45
Texas Pecan Cake, 47

CANDY
Potato Candy, 56

CASSEROLES
Baked Cheese Tomatoes, 53
Grits Casserole, 18
Hominy Grits Casserole, 20
Overnight Casserole, 16
Salmon Casserole, 49
Shrimp Louisiane Casserole, 37
Southern Illinois Hominy, 29
Monterey Bake, 52

COOKIES
Bourbon Balls, 22
Golden Cherry Chews, 36
Nut Cookies, 9
Oatmeal Cookies, 36
Pecan Crunch Cookies, 25
Persimmon Cookies, 36
Tassies, 36

FISH and SEAFOOD
Backyard Clambake, 15
Baked Fish, 26
Baked Whole Salmon, 51
Bayou Shrimp and Rice, 41
Cioppino, 44
Deviled Crab, 5
Deviled Crab, 14
Escalloped Oysters, 5
Fish Boil, 26

Fish Fillets in a package, 26
Fish Stew, 51
Halibut Amandine, 6
Hawaiian Shrimp, 59
Imperial Crab, 14
Jambalaya, 39
Little Salmon Pies, 51
New Orleans Stuffed Baked Fillets
    Creole, 40
Poached Salmon, 51
Salmonburgers, 61
Salmon Loaf, 51
Scallop Casserole, 5
Seafood Newburg, 14
Seafood Supreme, 39
Shrimp Creole, 45
Stuffed Baked Lobster, 6

FRUITS
Gala Fruit-Filled Melon, 23
Old-Fashioned Ambrosia, 25

ICE CREAM
Kumquat Ice Cream, 24
Lemon Dream Ice Cream, 60
Missouri Frozen Custard, 47

MEATS
Barbecued Short Ribs, 44
Barbecued Spareribs, 43
Broiled Venison Steak, 61
Brunswick Stew, 17
Care-Less Brisket of Beef, 50
Chili, 53
Cubed Beef Sauerbraten, 29
Frosted Corned Beef Loaf, 53
Hash Ranchero, 52
Hawaiian Ham Ring, 59
Hawaiian Ham Slices, 59
Mexican Meal, 41
Mex-Tex Tostados, 42
Milwaukee Grilled Dinner, 28
New Orleans Poor Boy Sandwich,
    39
Porcupine Meatballs, 19
Roll-Ups, 43
Spanish Enchiladas, 45
Stuffed Pork Chops, 28
Texas Pork Chops, 44
Venison Meat Loaf, 61

PANCAKES, etc.
New England Pancakes, 11
Old South Crackling Cakes, 18
Popovers, 10

PIES
Apple Butter Pie, 13
Apple Crisp, 55
Cherry-O-Cream Cheese Pie, 33
Cranberry Pie, 12
Cream Pie with Cherry Glaze, 32
Easy Coconut Cream Pie, 21
Egg Custard Pie, 33
French Silk Pie, 32
Fresh Blueberry Pie, 32
Fresh Gooseberry Pie, 55
Harrison Cream Pie, 32
Hawaiian Lemon Pie, 60

Maine Pumpkin Pie, 12
Maple Syrup Pie, 13
Montgomery Pie, 12
Peach Pie, 55
Pecan Pie, 21
Pennsylvania Dutch Shoofly Pie, 12
Pineapple Chiffon Pie, 21
Rhubarb Custard Pie, 33
Sour Cream Pie, 12

POULTRY
Arroz Con Pollo, 43
Baked Chicken Maryland, 16
Chicken Creole, 45
Chicken Olé, 44
Chicken Paprika with Spaetzles, 8
Chicken Pie, 16
Chicken Special, 52

PRESERVES
Corn Relish, 33
Cranberry Catsup, 61
Pear Chips Jam, 56
Rhubarb Jam, 33

PUDDINGS
Apple Cobbler, 10
Aunt Bertha's Indiana Persimmon
    Pudding, 35
Farm Pudding, 30
Graham Cracker Pudding, 30
Lemon Bread Pudding, 9
Maple Pudding, 9
New England Carrot Steamed
    Pudding, 8
New England Plum Pudding, 8
Peach Pudding, 54
Persimmon Pudding, 30
Southern Rice Pudding, 25
Sweet Potato Pudding, 25
Yakima Apple Pudding, 55

RICE, DUMPLINGS
Louisiana Boiled Rice, 40
Mama's Southern Dumplings, 18
Peanut Rice Roast, 20
Pepper Parsley Green Rice, 53

SAUCES
Barbecue Sauce, 39
Creole Sauce, 40

SOUPS
Charleston Okra Soup, 16
Chicken Soup New Orleans, 37
New England Fish Chowder, 5
Onion Soup Louisiana Style, 37
Pennsylvania Dutch Chowder, 3
Potato and Spinach Soup, 49
Potato Soup, 3

VEGETABLES
Baked Beans, 4
Baked Corn, 6
Beef and Beans, 52
Broccoli Bake, 20
Corn Pudding, 41
Creole Corn, 43
Fried Beans, 52
Okra, 40
Sauerkraut, 28
Southern Eggplant, 20
Stewed Okra Tomatoes, 53
Western Baked Beans, 52

ACKNOWLEDGMENT
Picture and recipe on Pages 15, 26-27,
58-59 and 62-63 used through the
courtesy of Reynolds Metals Company.